Crypto-Currency Mistak

Blockchain Education For Protecting You From Common Mistakes Made By Beginners

Lee Green

Respective authors own all copyrights not held by the publisher.

The information herein is offered for informational purposes solely and is universal as such. The presentation of the information is without a contract or any guarantee assurance. The trademarks used are without any consent, and the publication of the trademark is without permission or backing by the trademark owner. All trademarks and brands within this book are for clarifying purposes only and are owned by the owners themselves, not affiliated with this document.

Table of Contents

The Private Label E-Commerce Revolution [5 Books in 1]

Dropshipping Business Model on a Budget

The Complete Startup Crash Course

The Golden Ratio Trading Algorithm

Bookkeeping and QuickBooks Made Easy

The Private Label E-Commerce Revolution [5 Books in 1]

A Collection of Filters, Entertaining Topics and Viral Trends to Gain 10k Followers and Generate Passive Income

By

Lee Green

Table of Contents

Introduction

Don't think you can compete against millions of creators and influencers? Well, let's set one thing straight, not only can you do it but also how you can do it. Working smarter, not necessarily harder, makes all the difference.

This book is for those who wish to make a name of themselves by leaving behind a reputation, legacy on social media platforms. Or maybe, all you want is to be able to do what you love for a living and offer that to the world. Either way, you're in the right place.

If you haven't been able to make much of a passive income from these social platforms for a while now, you should know it's probably not you; it's the platform. This book aims toprovide an insight into these social platforms by teaching you how to increase your audience by changing some basic habits and teach you a few new tips, tricks, and tactics you can use by first understanding their working. 10,000 is perhaps the right number of followers to be considered literally as an influencer/brand, get paying offers, and raise your account's value.

It may be sluggish as you try to win the starting few followers, but it does get a little easier after that. Understanding the algorithm plays a crucial role in enlarging your audience. YouTube, Tik Tok, and Instagram use algorithms to recommend various creators. Once you understand how their algorithms work, you can easily reach a larger variety of users. By gaining an active audience of about 10K, YouTube, Tik Tok, and Instagram may consider paying attention to your content, and you could even gain more than 10,000 depending on your consistency.

Now, you are probably thinking "easier said than done", right? Well, don't worry, this book is solely there to make these things easier. To provide a how-to gain 10K followers quickly, An easy-to-use reference to aid your growth on social media platforms (i.e., YouTube, Tik Tok, and Instagram.)

Try not to read this book as a novel; rather, truly study it and apply it in your daily practices to notice change and improvement in your channel/account/profile growth.

First, this book will teach you why earning a passive income through YouTube, Tik Tok, and Instagram is the way to go, especially in this day and age, next, how each platform has its own way of working and different method to win over the platform to your side. And then, if you're having a tough time generating content for these platforms, the last part will teach you how you can remove your creativity block and let yourmuse come to you.Last but not least, Afterthoughts will give you that push you need to get cracking, radiating motivation and energy to really get you started.

CHAPTER I: Why it's One of the Best Ways to Earn

In current times, the Internet is available in almost every part of the world. People interact, learn, and enjoy through platforms. More specifically, YouTube, Tik Tok, and Instagram. Since 2020, most people have spent their time at home, and so usage of these social media platforms has grown excessively. People discovered hidden talents, curiosity, and inspiration so much more than before.

Even if people hadn't spent half their time on their phones or other electronic devices, there are so many advantages of working on YouTube, Tik Tok, and Instagram for a passive income.

1.1: Freedom of Speech

YouTube, Tik Tok, and Instagram are the kind of social media platforms that allow an individual to really do anything and everything they want, needless to say, as long as they follow community guidelines.

"I do not agree with what you have to say, but I'll defend to the death your right to say it." ~ Voltaire

From a thriller,a short film to kids toy reviews, from gameplays to reactions, whatever.These are platforms where even the smallest of people have a voice, and they can make it known. Your creativity can literally pay the bills and put food on the table. And there can always be an endless supply of creativity, that is if you know where to look.

What could you possibly want more than being able to do what you love for a living? It's the ideal dream.And there are so many advantages of being able to do what you enjoy for a living.

High Efficiency

You become more useful and productive with your work as you can be excited for the next day. Your work won't even feel like a job,and so you would find yourself more relaxed as it wouldn't feel like a burden, finding other things to do in your spare time would be exciting too.

Inspiration

When you're having a tough time, doing what you love can spark inspiration and motivation in you. Once you feel inspired, your ideas run like a high-qualitycar engine, and it can sometimes even get difficult to do all these amazing things you have in mind.

New Perspectives

When you are following a boring schedule every single day and spend most of your time thinking about what you would do once the weekends here, you should realize you're doing it wrong. When working on a social media platform, you don't have a boss; in fact, you are your own boss, much like running a business. You set timings that are best suited for your work, and as being a public figure is constantly exciting, you won't find yourself in the same routine each day. Sure, you would probably have some ups and downs, but at the end of the day, you work for your own satisfaction and so view life from a different point of view than those who work solely because they feel they have no choice.

Better Wellbeing

Working on your chosen niche on these social platforms sounds fun and enjoyable, and it is. What you probably didn't know that being happy is great for your health. In fact, it's a lot cheaper than being miserable and stressed for everyday of your life. It even relieves all that stress, mental and physical tension.

1.2: Fame

An Audience

Working on being a public figure or influencer gives you an audience that cares for you; they show an interest in your content. It could make you a role model for them, or they see your content to put a smile on their faces, it could help them in some basic struggles they didn't know they had until they saw your work.

Your followers/subscribers may value your opinions on certain topics and appreciates you and your content in the respective niche. And being validated for your effort would make anyone happy.

They even help you grow by giving honest feedback and so you can easily tell what it is they like about your content.

Opportunities

Fame grants you several chances to work with well-known brands or companies. Whether that be in sponsored advertisements or partnerships for products(i.e., perfume, apparel, electronic gadgets, games, etc.)

For example,maybe you're a sports-focused content creator, you could get offers from sportswear companies to model with their products!

Not only brands but also popular public figures would notice you, and you'd be given numerous opportunities to work with them, especially if you're in the same niche as them. When an already successful creator acknowledges and validates your content, they bring in their fans to your work, ultimately broadening your audience.

Forinstance, YouTuber Lilly Singh, also known as superwoman, grew so big on YouTube that she now hosts a late-night show called "A Little Late with Lilly Singh" on NBC. She not onlyreleased a film that entailed her world tour but also a book named "How to Be aBawse: A Guide to Conquering Life," which made it to New York Times best-seller list. She also won a substantial number of rewards on multiple award shows over the years and made her own music videos, and so much more.Her Niche? Entertainment.And it's an understatement to say she entertained.

@lilly with @malala Via Instagram

Of course, it didn't come easy to her, but with time, her channel grew and not only on YouTube but also across other platforms like Instagram.

Like her, once you obtain that loyal audience, you could try new things whenever you want, but not too much, or you may drive your audience away. You'd be able to work on creative projects. (i.e., Liza Koshy acted in a tv show and other showbiz related content, PewDiePe who made not one but two games with another company as well as a YouTube original show called "Scare PewDiePie", Joey Graceffa who made his own YouTube original show called "Escape the Night".)

1.3: Money

The obvious reason for earning through YouTube, Tik Tok, and Instagram? The Money.Succeeding on any social platform often promises good fortune. Influencers often buy new cars, houses, editors to help them with their work, maybe even a new oven!

You'd finally be able to finish that bucket list. Get something for the people you care about! And most importantly, once you get that money you've been waiting for, be grateful and don't take it for granted.

YouTubers like Lilly Singh made use of their money by making her profile a little more professional by hiring a team and basically becoming a CEO of her team. A lot of influencers do live charity streams, raise money, or donate for the poor and needy in several ways as well.Well, that's not all she did with her money she spent it for fun too as I'm sure you can as well do whatever you want with it.

Merchandising

You would be able to sell your own products, which would be your signature merch (people would recognize it as yours). Often influencers get sweatshirts, T-shirts, caps, posters, phone covers, etc. This increases your profits as well as advertising yourself. You get something to represent yourself with and receive more recognition.

CHAPTER II: YouTube

2.1: How it Works

To know how to easily get 10,000 subscribers on YouTube, you first need to be able to understand the YouTube software's working and how you can use it to your advantage.

Video

YouTube is a free space where creators can store videos, pictures, and posts. But their main focus is the videos that various people of all types upload. Google owns it, and its search engine is the second largest around the globe. YouTube videos can be embedded into other websites as well.

Moreover, YouTube recommends videos that are viewed by a similar audience to the one a user is currently watching.

Being successful through YouTube won't happen in a week. You have to be prepared to go through the rough patches as well as the smooth ones.

Analytics

There is a reporting, and self-service analytics tool on YouTube which provides intel regarding every video you upload so YouTube can help you easily keep track of how many views each video receives, what type of people are watching your content (age group, where they are from, and such).

It can provide data about:

1. The age groups and genders it is commonly seen by.

2. The statistics: comments, ratings, and views.

3. The countries your content is mostly seen in.

4. The first time your video was recommended to a user, either when they are watching something similar or when your video was recommended when they search a keyword.

5. In the first instance, your video was embedded in a website by a third party.

Advertising

YouTube embeds features that allow various businesses to promote their content to users who may have an interest in it, aiming at clients by subject and demographics.

The advertisers pay you each time someone in your audience views their Ad. They can decide the areas in which the Ad will show, the amount of payment, and the format.

Channels

Create your own niche, don't constantly jump from one genre to another, or your audience will never remain consistent.

2.2: The Content

Watch Time

Videos that consist of a higher watch time get recommended frequently on the main YouTube homepage. So how do you increase it? Pattern Interrupts.

These result in making your videos more vibrant, which prolongs the viewers' attention span.

A pattern interrupt can be jump cuts, graphics, different camera angles, and cheesy humor. It can put a smile on the watcher's face or catch them off guard, which keeps them watching.

Trends

Keeping up with the current times is vital for small channels to grow. Trends are one of the catalysts of increasing your audience.

PewDiePie Via YouTube

As of February 2021,most YouTubers stream live, do how-to tutorials, DIY's, etc.

Things like the chubby bunny challenge, Reddit reactions (cross-platform), spicy foods challenge, etc., gives more room for the creator and audience to get to know one another. The goal is to make them feel like your friend, so they feel comfortable enough to come back.

Create longer videos.

Making long videos (10+ minutes) actually gives your video a higher rank in YouTube's search results in most cases. Of course, if you make the video longer with not much to add, then it will still be lowly ranked as users will prefer not to waste their time.

And definitely avoid making videos longer than an hour because it's likely the viewers' attention gets diverted.

Like, Share, and Subscribe

At any point of the video, remind your viewers to subscribe, but make sure you don't keep mentioning that along with 'Like, Share, and hit the notification bell' as this tends to irritate the viewers due to the fact that they just want to watch the video. Keep the message short and maybe even humorous to attract the viewers.

Link more videos at the end.

If the users watch more of *your* content, they will probably subscribe. So, promoting your videos will definitely increase the chances of them watching it as it would be convenient for them to just click on that instead of going to your channel and surfing through there.

Quality over Quantity

Viewers can never be fooled by the number of videos you upload every week, they value the effort and time put into each piece of content, and they are well aware that you are as human as they are.

Do try maintaining a schedule just to let your viewers know when they can expect a video, but don't force it, or it will not be valued.

Thumbnail and Video Title

Your thumbnails should be eye-catching and interesting, as it is the first thing they see when they are introduced to your channel. It's your first impression. Make sure it's a high-quality image.

If it's a professional website, a simple and sleek thumbnail will do. If it's a vlog or an entertainment purpose video, an exciting title with an image of the most important part of the video in place of the thumbnail would fit nicely.

For example, if you want to give your review on a certain product, give a strong statement as a title that would be intriguing for people to watch (i.e., 'Why I think the new Tesla cars are amazing', 'Why Harry Potter actually makes no sense', 'Public Speaker Reacts to PewDiePie')

More Content

At the end of your videos, hint at what you'll be doing next so your viewers can come back for more.

Keep track of your subscriber magnet. In analytics, creators can see what type of videos made by you have the most views. So, start by focusing on those. Obviously, don't make a hundred parts on the same topic, but keeping track of your subscriber magnet can help a lot.

2.3: Channel Profile

Keep an attractive and creative Channel with intriguing art styles, so it shows the work put in your banner. It welcomes the viewers. Here are some examples:

Jaclyn Lovey Via YouTube: here,Jaclyn made a minimalistic banner with her video update schedule and her genre of videos mentioned, so newcomers do not have to search for it; convenience.

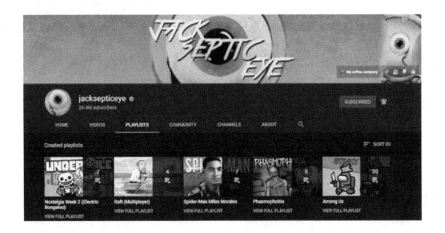

jacksepticeye Via YouTube: Jack, a successful YouTuber with over 20 Million views, categorized all his videos in playlists so users can access any genre of his videos anytime. Also, notice a signature logo, and he mentioned all his handles, brand links too.

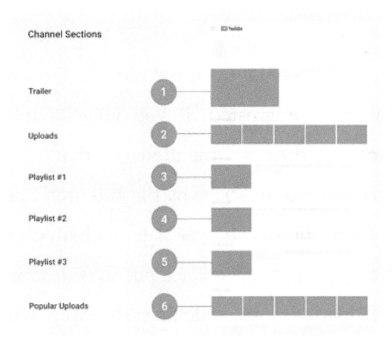

Make an exciting and persuading channel trailer. Preferably short and catchy, show the best you can here because these viewers came specifically to your channel, and you want to keep them there.

Organize the Channel page in a way that's convenient to the viewers.

Check out this basic layout:

Mention other platforms you use so they keep up with you if they don't rely on YouTube.

In 'About', make sure you provide at least 300 words about yourself, what kind of content you put out into the world, and why you think they'd be interested. If you have an upload schedule (please do), then mention that as well. Persuade the viewers to subscribe by the end of it. Keeping a polite tone in your descriptions, whether it be a channel description or video description, gives the viewer a positive and kind tone. They wouldn't particularly enjoy watching someone who talks in a manner of giving orders rather than guiding or entertaining (depending on your content subject).

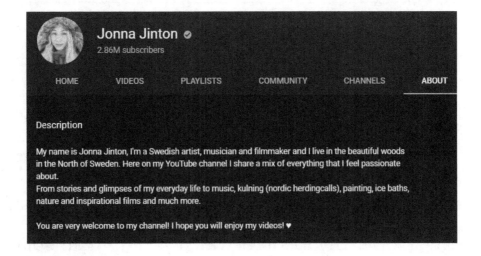

Make sure you use well-known keywords that describe your content. (i.e., Crash courses, funny, motivational, etc.) so the YouTube algorithm can detect these things. Here's an easy comparison:

A:

Via YouTube

B: Via YouTube

Which is a better Description of the YouTuber? I hope you say B, because it is, in fact, B.

Categorize your videos into playlists. For example, if you are running a gaming channel, make sure long gameplays are divided into separate videos but put together in one playlist after you upload them. Not many people watch 4-hour gameplays all at once, especially when you are starting as a small channel. But suppose you divide your gameplays into videos and edit them to cut out the boring bits. In that case, they may enjoy watching multiple short videos, which would be around 15-20 minutes each- depending on your preferences.

2.4: Interactivity

Replying to comments is the best and simplest way to gain more subscribers. The more you interact with your viewers and give importance to their feedback, the longer they stay.

"When creators take the time to interact with their local community, it can encourage audience participation and ultimately result in a larger fanbase." ~ YouTube.

Creator Hearts- you can heart your favorite comments to recognize comments from your public. By doing this, the viewer gets a notification, and this keeps interactivity high by leading them back to your channel. These notifications receive 300% additional clicks than normal.

Once you get a handful of people that are consistent in watching your content, you can even ask for their opinion on anything related to the video or even an idea for the next video. To engage yourcommunity is perhaps the most important thing, especially when you are a growing channel. Doing Q&A videos every once in a while acknowledges the audience and engages them more.

Recently, YouTube updated, and now Creators can interact with their audience with polls and posts as well as comments. Using these frequently to keep your audience there is vital.

Shine Theory

Needless to say, they'd be more excited by a famous YouTuber replying to their comments, but you could be famous soon enough too! So, building a community that promotes each other does help. This concept comes from the Shine Theory.

Shine Theory is a long-term investment, where two individuals, creators, or consumers, help each other by means of advertising or engagement depending on the platform it is being used.

CHAPTERIII:Tik Tok

3.1: Down the Rabbit Hole

Over 2 billion people have downloaded Tik Tok all around the globe. Especially during the global pandemic, literally, everyone seems to have this app on their phone- and even if they don't have the app, it is taking over the apps they *do* have.

Tik Tok is super addicting, and the main reason for this is that each video is no longer than one minute, which gives viewers quick entertainment /tips /motivation.

Tik Tok famous is a word the vast majority seems to be throwing around as if it is a solid career, but the problem is, they all act as though it's a comfortable ride without even putting their back into it! Though it's a little more complicated than that, and you'd know that. But don't worry, here's a step-by-step guide to how you can be Tik Tok famous in no time.

This is the kind of platform that anyone can get into, from a 7-year-old to a 70-year-old *anyone*. Most people follow overnight after one of your Tik Tok's go mega-viral. Without further ado, let's start with all the things you need to remember to get 10 000 followers on Tik Tok.

3.2: The Algorithm

The Tik Tok algorithm was updated recently at the start of 2021, due to which a number of views on Tik Toks have started to go down. They did this because Tik Tok realized Tik Toks could go viral for almost anyone and a lot of creators' content was against community guidelines, so the early adopter advantage is lost. A way to tackle this is- keep pumping out more content. These algorithms will keep updating throughout the years, but the best you can do is give the viewers a reason to watch.

3.3: Your Profile

Username

Choose a simple yet unique username. One that is familiar to your niche would be most preferred as it would make users find you conveniently. (i.e., if your Tik Toks are travel-focused, you can call yourself JourneysInLife)

Bio

Think of an intriguing Profile Bio. Something welcoming, relatable, original, fun, and interesting your followers would enjoy. And definitely mention your niche to clarify your target audience. Often really good bios consist of a call to action (i.e., follow for a cookie).

Upload a Photo (high-quality image not to look cheap). Link your other social media handles like Instagram, YouTube, etc.

3.4: The Content

Target Audience

Before blindly making videos, you need to consider what kind of audience you're aiming for. Firstly, they use Tik Tok. If you think editing videos the same way you'd edit a YouTube or IGTV video will work, you're wrong. Every platform is unique in its own significant way,so you need to pay attention to how Tik Tok is entertaining and focuses on that.

Is it family-friendly content for youngsters? Short tutorials for artists? Perhaps it's professional cooking for beginners. You need to think about your audience's geolocation, age group, gender, so on and so forth.

This is an approximate age breakdown:

- Age 55+: 5%

- Age 44-53: 2%

- Age 34-43: 7%

- Age 24-33: 15%

- Age 17-23: 41%

- Age 13-16: 26%

What's your Niche?

Delivering high-quality videos (in both quality of the video and content) is the most basic important thing. Don't steal content from other underrated creators, or it will have dire consequences like getting banned.

Make it unique, edit your videos with your ability if you can because people get tired of seeing the same editing design used by the Tik Tok app. There are various editing apps like ViaMaker, Zoomerang, Quik, InShot, Funimate, etc.

Quality

You need a really powerful hook in the first 3 seconds the keep the viewers wanting to watch more. Your job is to do everything and anything to keep the viewers from clicking away then make them interested enough to follow!

To do this, you need a significant number of pattern interrupts-graphics, different camera angles, etc. It could be as easy as starting with a greeting or as concrete as taking the time to explore or finishing your wish list. A trend disrupts you to exciting new locations, both visually and psychologically. It jolts you away from your comfortable perceptions and rituals and then into broad freedom of possibilities.

Better quality videos are pleasing to the eye, and they will likely continue watching until it ends. Sometimes Tik Tok degrades your videos' quality, and the reason this happens is thatthe data saved on your app has been turned on often than naught. This feature is on means the Tik Tok application downloads your mobile data while you watch videos. This decreases the resolution of your clips too. So, to tackle this, you can turn off the data saver feature.

Collabs

Collaborating with some people you have good chemistry with really improves shares as it would be increasing both your and the other Tik Tokers views/follows another branch of Shine Theory.

Not just that, but Tik Tok allows you to reply to other influencers Tik Tok with your own, right? Use that! Make your reply unique and interesting to get them and other viewers to notice.

When it comes to collaborations with companies, sponsorships sound nice but try not to overdo it. While looking for new celebrities to partner with, be sure to review how many supported videos are posted. When a majority of their latest material is paying for updates, their commitment rate will not last. Alternatively, search for influencers with a decent amount of organic, non-sponsored material. As they probably have fans interested and involved.

Going Viral

When you post a video on Tik Tok, your creativity has the potential to ignite a chain reaction.

To get a decent amount of exposure, engage in trends, challenges, and duets. Put your own twists on patterns that captivate individuals. Paying attention to and bookmarking popular clips can prove useful to use it for inspiration. In Tik Tok, there are so many viral challenges. Engaging in various challenges will increase your visibility to the network and encourage you to get far more follows.

On the majority of your Tik Toks, for now, at least, use recommended and trending songs. Positive content almost always has more views, something quirky and enjoyable with a warm tone. Using a trending song is the next move (except when your music is original or a video idea in particular to a kind of sound.)

This is the reason why using trending songs is clever: basically, Tik Tok is a little wired in regard to trending songs to promote videos. It wasn't a random occurrence that Tik Tok also works with record companies; they work together to promote the artist's music in the app to improve the sales of the album and raise the likelihood that the song can hit the top rankings. Tik Tok practically dominates the music world. A mere peek at the week's Top 100 tunes. Most of those best hits on Tik Tok are those that are mega-famous. How do you know what tunes everyone's listening to? Simply choose one of the suggested tracks the platform recommends when you make your film.

Get on top of all those trends, except with a surprise. Do the idea of popular dances or rising clips, but add a twist on it and make it something of your own. You need to balance trending videos with fresh material when you're a small producer. A Tik Tok clip received millions of views, and that account got about 10,000 Tik Tok followers; it just happened overnight.

However, once you receive those views, you shouldn't anticipate the next day to be filled with that much fame, because you will probably be disappointed. Once you get over a million views, then you need to keep up the work or probably work even harder than before to keep everyone there.

Make sure you don't take part in really cringe trends, though!

Using Hashtags

Utilize hashtags as much as you can, especially hashtags that are trending. This actually matters because the Tik Tok algorithm detects these hashtags and recommends your content accordingly.

The cleverer and simpler your hashtags are, the higher your videos get ranked on Tik Tok, which in result increases your views and likes. Along with being in contact with record labels, Tik Tok often works with companies/brands, and their drives are almost always attached with a hashtag. This encourages your videos on people's For You Page during the duration of the campaigns.

1-2 hashtags are preferred. Go to the Discover tab and take 1-2 trending and 1-2 broad hashtags or tags related to your related to you exclusively and trendy.

Most Popular: #tiktokers #lfl #bhfyp #follow #explorepage #followforfollowback #explore #meme #tiktokdance #viral #memes #tiktokindia #photography #tiktokindonesia #k #cute #art #youtube #instagood #fashion #likes #bhfyp #likeforlikes #trending #music #funny#tiktok #instagram #love #like **Timing Matters!**

What time you decide to post your content actually matters. When most people are online is when you'd want to put out videos and this depends on your geolocation heavily. If you're careful, you can get twice the followers you'd normally get.

Posting late at night (not too late), afternoon, and early morning tend to be the best times as most people would be looking through their phones then.

But that's just an average. To be more specific, go into your account analytics and content section, look at the past 7 days and what times your content was viewed most often, then make your posting times according to when your most interactive followers were active to make it as convenient for them as possible. Also, take into consideration the timings more well-known Tik Tokers in your niche are posting.

Repost and Share.

Sometimes, your video doesn't do as well the first time but reposting it several times a day and week can drastically change that because sometimes your followers just miss it. Saying things like 'Posting again till it goes viral' or 'Reposting since it didn't do too well last time' can really make a difference.

Sharing your videos on every other social media platform (i.e., Instagram, Twitter, Facebook, etc.)

Engagement

You need to turn your viewers, commenters, and likers into followers, especially at such an early stage. Basically, your early squad needs the spa treatment. To do this, perhaps the most important thing is engaging with your community. Interacting with them as much and as often as you can is vital to Tik Tok's growth.

Credits: wired

Reply to each and every comment.People love viewing comments seeing their opinion was acknowledged would be a satisfying feeling foreveryone. Follow everyone, and I mean everyone that has interacted with your account in anyway.

Go Live every single day, and it really boosts your page. Even if you're super busy, go live and work!

If you receive hate comments, reply back with a bit of humor! However, if it's constructive criticism, show interest, and try actually considering their opinion, this can really help your account develop.

Ask questions in your videos, so they feel the need to reply in the comments. This is a little trick most creators use.

Staying Consistent

Posting regularly is important. Post multiple times a day (considering the timings) and try avoiding uploading content right after each other, or it will not be pushed to the For You page.

Stockpile videos: If you have a day off, film as much content as you can so you can still upload videos if you're too busy another day. Posting 3-6 times a day is an ideal amount.

Duration

The duration of each video is preferred to be 11-17 sec long. The ideal time for something to be pushed out into the algorithm. And you'd get a good amount of watch time. Keep it shorter than you think it needs to be.

Tik Tok revolves around fun and concise videos, so if yours is too long than they would like, Tik Tok may decrease your rank on the For You page.

Ask them to follow, like, and comment.

The easiest method to improve the number of followers you have is by asking the viewers to 'double tap!' or 'let me know what you think in the comment section'; these things remind viewers to give you some sort of feedback on the content you create.

Asking for engagement in every video for a *very* brief period of time in the video and saying it in the description is important. Make sure it isn't mentioned for longer than 2-3 seconds, or the viewer will get bored and click away.

Keep all your content accessible.

Never delete any of your Tik Tok videos because it's likely your posts won't do well right away; you need to give it time. Your previous posts can go viral any time, so never keep them private or delete them.

There have been many times a Tik Toker posts a video, and it gets hardly 500 views in the first night, but about a few weeks later, it starts to become trending again, and you get a thousand more views.

Judge Yourself

Not to the point, you put yourself down, of course, but realistically judging yourself to keep track of your work is important.

How will this video contribute to your growth?

Is it interesting for people in my own niche?

Why would it be interesting?

What themes can I use to make this better?

If the most popular Tik Toker in my niche saw this, would they be impressed?

Take these things into consideration when you're done with certain Tik Toks.

Follow Guidelines

Especially with the recent 2021 update, you don't want to get on Tik Tok's bad side. Make sure you aren't copying someone else's work on your own profile, as that would really degrade your account.

Funded partnerships may not be as clear to Tik Tok as they are to other social networking sites, but that wouldn't imply that the very same FTC laws do not apply. Tik Tok celebrities are expected to report advertising with a transparent and obvious message that the material is funded or promoted.

Do not, under any circumstance, attempt to get free followers. This will never help you really grow. And it can have really adverse consequences later on if you are serious about Tik Tok as this is seen as a way to steal from Tik Tok. Trying to buy free followers will never get you the triumph you thrive for.

Stitch- The Tik Tok Feature

This adds yet another way for the user to interact with material that is created and posted every day by the creative Tik Tok users. Stitch is a feature the company called which enables a user to put in snippets of another Tik Tok video in yours.

How can you use it?

1. Search for the video you want to stitch and then click on 'Send to'.

2. Click on 'Stitch'

3. You can pull only 5 seconds out of the video, so choose wisely.

4. Make the rest of the video you want to put in with the stitched snippet.

5. Stitch them all together!

In the settings menu, you may select if you want to allow others to stitch your material. This is accessible on the Security and Confidentiality tab underneath "Settings and Privacy." You could allow or remove Stitch for any of your clips. Conversely, this feature can be customized for every clip you post.

Stay Stress-free

Don't try to push out more content forcefully, if your audience sees that you are, they would easily be able to get that your content came from a negative mindset. Keep it fun, enjoy making the clips, actually show your positivity.

Having a healthy mindset further nurtures your creativity and gets your ideas flowing, and you need as much of that as possible. Being authentic with your followers is key.

A few different tactics that have proved effective, such as constructive self-discuss and positive envisioning, can achieve encouraging thought.

Here are a few tactics that would prove beneficial for you to prepare your brain in thinking positively to get you started with generating content.

Concentrate on the good stuff. A part of our life is inconvenient situations and obstacles. Look at the constructive stuff once you're faced with one, regardless of how minor or relatively meaningless they are. You may still discover the ultimate positive aspect of any inconvenience if you search for it, even if it's not readily apparent.

Train with appreciation. Studying kindness has been shown to alleviate depression, boost self-esteem and promote endurance in some very trying situations. Image friends, experiences, or stuff that give you any type of warmth or delight, and struggle to convey your thanks at least once every day. This could be a thank you to a co-worker for assisting with a job, to a significant one for cleaning dishes, or to your cat for the affection they have provided.

Keep a diary of thanks. Research studies have reported that putting down stuff you're thankful for will boost your motivation and your state of wellness. You could do that by writing in a thankful diary daily or by setting down a range of items that you're happy for the days when you're going through a rough time. Using this to generate ideas even if it's really far-fetched should prove useful.

Find your motivation, whether that be intrinsic or extrinsic. You get to create the kind of content you like on Tik Tok, any kind! Use that as your passion and drive to work harder and do better.

Let's take a look at a few Tik Tokers

Daniel here has already made 10 parts of the same category and he still has millions of views. Why? Because he doesn't do the *same thing each* time of course, he changes it up, builds better for the next parts. His idea is original, unique, and entertaining!

But be careful not to overdo it, you can't go making 50 parts of the same theme as that would really just stretch it out too much and no one enjoys a guest who overstays their welcome.

daniel.labelle ✓ Daniel LaBelle

If people lagged. Part 10

♫ original sound - Daniel LaBelle

2.9M

16.3K

50.8K

daniel.labelle Via TikTok

Zach shows a clip of the most absurd idea there is: fishing in your house, using these surprises and then a pattern interrupt which involves him falling into the water really is an odd sight to see though very entertaining and unique.

Because of this, a large number of people shared his video and commented in it to share their thoughts.

zachking Via TikTok

CHAPTER IV: Instagram

4.1: About You

Instagram is used by everyone in almost every part of the world. It's so popular because Instagram uses imagery rather than text, and people are extra quick to respond to that. It's easier to understand and process visual data rather than heaps of words. And so, visual marketing is blowing up.

The main focus on Instagram is are images. Captions are put out of the way and under the image for that exact reason.

Portrait photography is perhaps the most popular amongst the flock of imageries on Instagram. And most of these images are almost always edited by third-party applications (i.e., Snapseed, VSCO, Adobe Photoshop Express, Polarr).

Not just images, but also Boomerangs, IGTV videos, filters (of which most are created by users), stories, etc. These things push engagement to the front lines.

Naturally, every time Instagram's algorithm changes, it impacts every person who accesses it. You need to make sure youaren't going against the current of those waves. Becausethe fact is that their algorithm is constantly judging posts all over the globe and deciding which users can see each moment they open the app.

Instagram's algorithm works on machine learning, which makes the way your posts are ranked constantly changing. This book has the most recent details about how to deal with the algorithm to push you further in the marketing campaign and to keep developing engagement with your followers.

Ever since Instagram halted the inverted response in 2016, each specific feed on the site has been arranged as per the algorithm's guidelines.

As per the official @creators handle of Instagram, this concluded in a pleasant result for everybody. Basically, saying they won't be changing it back.

4.2: Ranking Factors

Genre/Niche

Design your account, configure it in a way people can know precisely what they can expect from you. After which, you post intriguing content that your audience will enjoy instantly. If people have liked those kinds of posts before, the system is much more likely to display them.

For example, Let's say Steven came in contact with a verified account. He will probably see more posts from that account, especially if he saw more content from there.

Simply put, users who communicatewith content similar to yours are probably going to come across your account as well.

Timing

Recent posts are always going to be recommended more than others. So,just like Tik Tok, posting in timing when your followers are normally active is vital.

People who spend over an hour scrolling on Instagram are obviously going to see numerous kinds of posts from top to bottom compared to someone who spends hardly a few minutes will only see only the top-ranked ones.

Instagram portrays the best at the top of users' feed every time the user activates the application. So, someone who follows hundreds of thousands of accounts will most likely miss a fair number of posts from people they are even really close to.

Engaging Your Audience

Just like every other social media platform, Instagram wishes for users to stay on the app as much and as long as possible as long as they are interested. As anend result, the software cranks up profiles in which the followersare already conversing. This guarantees that the stress on community participation is essential for advertisers and developers.

Credits: mavsocial.com

Sliding in DMs, tagging one

another in blogs, and consistently posting comments all are acts thatimply a strong bond among users as well as likes, shares, and views.

4.3: What You Need toDo

Pay Attention.

Seeing your Instagram stats is, perhaps shockingly, a few of the easiest ways to get insight into not only how your viewers think but also how the application looks at you.

Could you send everyone much of the same, or twists on the subject? Will they want better photos or videos? Just how many views come from hashtags? What kind of content is going to wow the audience?

Insights tell you did well, so it's up to you to work out where to run from that performance.

Keep It Coming

Some type of involvement, and figuring out where the intended crowd is. To have a grip on the Instagram algorithm, you have to create bonds with your followers first. And because the volume is simple to compute and accomplish than performance, the first item on the agenda is to create a social media posting schedule to stay on track.

What is consistency? Mean for Instagram? This is exclusive to your niche. As you just started, start with the way you want to progress. Think about what's affordable for the team to create.

If you draw viewers with a spark, three stories, two posts, and one IGTV video per day produced a certain amount of perception. Volume and layout selections would depend on the resources you currently have. And what's most critical, however, is to concentrate on publishing posts that you feel proud of regularly.

Reposting is Key.

Even after you have a nice schedule, you're following and knowing what your followers expect, pushing content out into the world isn't simple like butter on jam.Recycle, change-up your best work. Now, not only do you know Instagram wants it, but it also saves a lot of time.

You could transform the videos to gifs, similar pictures to a slideshow,and use pictures used in another photo shoot for multiple reasons, throwbacks, and repost on stories.

Just use the same thing but be extra creative with it.

Collaborating withOther Influencers& Brands

Keep an eye on what other public figures in your niche are up to, and if possible, try to do a collab with them.

Perhaps the easiest way to naturally broaden your scope to fresh eyes is to seek a suitable friend with a complimentary following while still attracting the viewers' interest with appropriate different perspectives.The outcome may very well provide an added strength from Instagram if the partnership is as enjoyable for your community as it would be for you.

Though you need to make surethat the person you choose to partner with is suitable and legitimate, as other influencers will judge you based on who you collab with, it is probably best if you do a detailed background check before setting a collab date with them.

As that influencer will be bringing in their audience, you need to see what kind of followers they have and their analytics. Making sure you don't bring in the wrong crowd who would go away as soon as they came. You could check this by looking at their engagement on posts. If the person you are intending to collab with is genuine and interactive with his/her audience, you should probably go for it.

As searching through every single person, you could collab with would take a significant amount of time, you could use means likeNinjaoutreach, Meltwater, GroupHigh, Newswire, Cision Communications Cloud, etc.This software allows you to make your listing in its database, making things a lot more convenient for you as time is, in fact, of the essence.

The kinds of sponsorships you could get fall into three basic categories: large accounts (120K followers) get at least $400 per sponsored post, middle-class (3K-100K followers) get at least $150, and small accounts (less than 3K)get around $100 or less.

After making a list of the sponsorships you'd like to go for, you need to send each one your pitch. But not in the first text, of course, that would be not polite. Tell them why you're interested in the subject they put out and communicate with them. Once you know what they want exactly, you could develop an amazing pitch.

Next, you need to plan your influencer publicizing campaign. Makesure you keep interacting with the influencers so you can get an insight into what they think. Consider other people's opinions to make a master plan using the influencers and your creativity.

As soon as you have initiated your campaign, please keep track of how it's doing and keep adjusting it accordingly.

An example:

@omayazein partnered up with a brand calledModanisa and gave her audience a discount code, which in turn gets a lot of shares, and she has about 1 Million followers!

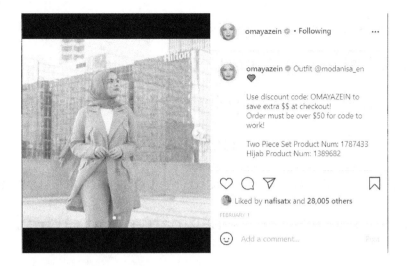

@omayazein Via Instagram

Reward Them

As discussed before, Instagram values engagement A LOT, so give your audience what they want! When your audience shares your posts on story or DM, comments and likes push your posts to the top instantly.

The goal should be to create a kind of commitment and passion that motivates individuals to advocate and empower themselves. The service could do the job for you if you already have an outstanding Business-to-consumer service. Anything other than that, you would need to find means of subtly encouraging individuals.

Please stop posting everything sent to you from your community. Compile the latest and integrate material into the digital plan of your content whenever appropriate. And bear in mind that merely reposting the stories of other users has also been specifically noted as something that would not include your stories on the Explore List, so make sure you remain imaginative and on topic.

Like your followers' and viewers' comments, reply to each one, even the haters. Try getting into a conversation with them. Interact with them through stories, polls, use trending filters.

Ask questions on your stories and share them, be humorous, genuine, everything and anything interesting. It could be 'what's your opinion on....' Or 'what's your most embarrassing story!', etc.

If they reply to your stories, make sure you reply!! And not after days at a time, but as soon as you can. Enjoy your time with them. Really try and understand what they wish to see from you. Unless they're just there to hate on you, then you should probably ignore it or if you could do something creative with it (while following community guidelines), go for it.

Follow influencers that are familiar with your niche. This can link other people that are interested in your type of content to you. Not just follow, but also like and comment on their posts, share it! (Another way of utilizing the Shine theory). Showing interest in other people's content can help you too.

Use the Hashtag System

Just like Tik Tok, hashtags are an important part of Instagram. It is the middleman between you and the right audience. It's the lowest building block, especially when you're just starting out.

If you think using heaps of hashtags, including ones that do not correlate with your niche, will help, you might be wrong. It would be misusing the hashtag system, and that leads you to a direct road to the bad side of Instagram because they do, in fact, notice those who try abusing the algorithm. And not to mention, you are not gaining anything by trying to show it to people who have no interest in your niche.

The maximum quantity of hashtags you are allowed to use is 30 per post, and yes, use all those 30. Try writing those hashtags in the first comment rather than in the caption, so it looks a bit more well put together.

Perhaps not all hashtags that you assume are nice would be suitable for your own use. It is why every last one of you would want to verify to see whether the material is important to your subject.

When deciding whether a hashtag is right for your post, there are two key considerations to have a look at Niche and Dimension.

Never use only the most famous and vague hashtags, thinking you would be able to reach a larger crowd because you won't. You'll just be a hidden needle in a haystack. An invisible need at that. Why? Because they aren't specific enough, and a lot of popular influencers already use those so you wouldn't be too noticed yet.

Please make sure you have certain hashtags that you use in every post (with fewer follows) so that you can be noticed by at least one familiar audience (needless to say, they need to be your target audience too).

It would be best if you would be able to find a middle ground between hashtags that not one soul has ever heard of before and hashtags that everyone knows about. Both would reward you little. Try hashtags that have about 90,000-900,000 post range.

Sorry, But Buying Is NOT the Way to Go

You can purchase double-taps or follows in due to despair just to see whether a lift is what they needed to get moving all along. But while this may make you appear popular to random people; it couldn't be farther from the facts.

Finally, they consider giving up both as a waste of time on Instagram and stop bringing in any considerable effort to expand, since they just do not see what else there is to do. Don't purchase likes, fans, and also, don't try the old trick of interaction pods.

Yes, even Instagram notices it if you buy followers/likes/views. Not only Instagram but also your followers. Which makes things a lot worse. And so, you won't gain any kind of income from that.

Using Highlights

Utilize the highlights feature and make/or find suitable cover photos for each to maintain consistency.It is making a profile that's pleasing to the eye and fitting for your niche and target audience.

4.4: Seeing is Believing

You may think this is all talk and no action, so let's drive that notion away by looking at a few of the many influencers on Instagram.

Notice the overall layout of this account. The username and profile instantly tell the users what the account is about.

Just the username would do this for us too but @wedarkacademia further described what it was about as well as threw in a bit of personality to the description as well as handles for other social platforms.

Their posts are consistent and related to one another. See the Highlights categorized neatly too.

@wedarkacademia Via Instagram

Responses like these encourage so much growth and engagement amongst the target audience.

@jonnajinton Via Instagram

@madeyemoodswing interacting with their audience. Their username being humorous and instantly getting the attention of Harry Potter fans who understand the reference.

Drawing in users of various kinds though if @madeyemoodswing doesn't involve any kind of Harry Potter related content, those fans may lose interest.

@madeyemoodswing Via Instagram

Jonna Jinton, blogging her art, photography and life on Instagram whilst also mentioning that she works on another platform (YouTube). Her posts are coherent and in sync with nature and mostly winter in her home country.

Her description and highlights are simple and straight to the point which a lot of users would find convenient and contemporary.

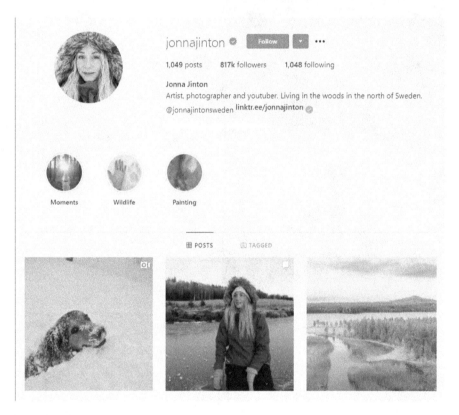

@jonnajinton Via Instagram

CHAPTER V: Ideas for Newbies

5.1: Idea Generation

There is not much to implement without ideas, and since the implementation is the secret to progress, creative ideas are required to enable some sort of change. It is clear that thoughts alone are not going to make creativity possible, since you need to be able to construct a structured mechanism to handle such innovations. The concept is not only about producing lots of it but also about bringing care to the nature of it.

It's not easy to create grade A content 24/7. Often people find it difficult to break out of their usual routine and habits when thinking about working on something new. In order to get out of the negative spiral, you need to glance at the development of creativity altogether and incorporate a few of the most key factors, strategies, and procedures that could be used more routinely to produce fresh concepts.

Perhaps you need original thoughts so a new possibility can be thoroughly explored?

Maybe you are trying to find a new way of solving a creativity barrier, or are you hoping for a decent answer to the dilemma?

Why does it matter?

Generating ideas is the outcome ofcreating complex, tangible, or conceptual theories. It's at the top of the funnelfor concept organization, which works on seeking potential alternatives to true or suspected challenges and possibilities.

Ideas are, as stated, the very first move into change. Fresh theories rely on you progressing as independent individuals. From the point of view of a person, whether you feel stuck with a job or otherwise unable to resolve that one dilemma, fresh solutions will motivate you to push ahead.

The aim of fresh concepts is to reinforce the manner in which you work, irrespective of your priorities or the kinds of things you're searching for.

To fuel productivity and improve nature on a broader scale, societies rely on creativity. Creativity improves emerging innovations and enterprises. They are providing creators with more opportunities.

How do you do it?

Chances are, you brainstorm. However, it's been found that brainstorming requires more time and tends to fewer ideas as ofplanning, logging, and managing the meeting would take a lot more time than it should. While there are certain approaches to boost the quality of brainstorming, it's preferred if brainstorming isn't your first thought.

Nevertheless, certain methods are worth taking a look at. As you're searching for various kinds of ideas, it is beneficial to have methods in mind that help in developing them. Several of these concept development approaches may be used for further productive brainstorming and another creativity type.

5.2: The Techniques

Challenging proposals

This concept is when you bring an issue or opportunity into view due to the possibility of innovatively solving it. It can let you make a certain doubt about your content and aim it at your audience to get more ideas and useful opinions after you have identified what you intend to gain from it.

These idea challenges come in handy, especially when you're looking to engage a large audience of up to 10000. When you plan an idea challenge, pre-define the outcomes you'd like, the niche, followers, subscribers, etc. Make sure you keep track of the time with this technique to make sure it's working.

Similarities

You can use data and statistics from previous posts or videos on social media platforms to improve on ideas for another piece of content; this is thinking simultaneously.It is the simplest way of generating fresh content as it's often experimented with and succeeded.

In Example, YouTuber's making reaction videos continually but of various kinds of content.

SCAMPER

This method applies critical thinking to alter creativity, which is already present — adjusting open-sourceideas to improve and agree on the best answer.

1. Substitution – Your old content being substituted with others to gain improvement.

2. Combining- Merging two or more ideas into one master idea for your content.

3. Adapting- Evaluates the options to make a method more versatile and works on the design, system, or principle alongside other related gradual changes.

4. Modification- From a broader context, changing not only the concept but also changing the concept looks at the challenge or potential and tries to change the outcomes.

5. Improvising by putting to another use- Searching for opportunities to use the concept or current content for some other reason and, if applicable to other areas of your profile or channel, analyzes the potential advantages.

6. Elimination- This technique studies all the possibilities, and if you find more than one fragment was removed.

7. Reversal- The emphasis of this procedure is to reverse the order of factors that can be swapped of your idea.

This technique was originatedfrom the idea of brainstorming, but it applies to your thinking technique too. If you make generating ideas a daily activity by a series of trivial things, you could have a decent chance of winning the main breakthrough. Occasionally all it takes is really to reflect on what you already have. Sometimes, creators want to worry about the next remarkable thing being discovered. It is easy to overlook that the endless gradual changes are the aspects that can have a difference in the medium haul while creating fresh concepts. As a baseline, utilizing your existing theories or methods will explain a lot in relation to your present content, and that is what the SCAMPER strategy is really about.

Reverse Psychology

This method will make you challenge your content-related perceptions. Reverse thinking comes in handy when you feel you are trapped in the traditional mentality, and it appears to be impossible to come up with such unique ideas. It helps in checking our routinely-habits as the answer to finding more content isn't always a straight-to-the-point road. You consider the possibilities of what the opposite would do for your profile or channel, even if you end up thinking of the most peculiar of solutions.

5.3: Once You've Got It

Organizing Ideas

Once you've got all those ideas down, planning and organizing them can be difficult if you don't know where to start. Creators need to collect this creativity as soon as it comes to them instead of using it as soon as it comes up.

Jotting down all your ideas in a notebook or on your phone can be helpful, and most people do this as it's only for personal use. But if you wish for other people's opinions on the matter to know their judgment, this could be a hassle. Not to worry though, there are things like idea management tools to aid you with that.

Management

A concept tool for effective functions as the foundation of the method of idea planning. This is how you can assemble the ideas, analyze them, debate, prioritize them, take account of their success, and the overall course of the operations of your idea generation.

Since concept planning is such a huge subject and famous influencers or public figures are likely to have loads of suggestions, it often makes perfect sense for most influencers or creators to use a designated idea management system.

It is just as productive to handle ideas with a designated method as the underlying mechanism at the back end. You could create a mechanism that makes it a lot easier to produce and refine fresh concepts and create ideas a persistent practice. The methods that are too confusing can infuriate people, so try not to make things too difficult.

5.4: Winning at Creativity

The Appropriate Crowd

It is necessary to include the right individuals in the equation for the content to be as efficient as possible. Start engaging all influencers who know about the content creation and are sincerely involved in you making a difference.

Ensure your community is the target audience and well educated on the topic if the aim is to involve a wider community of users to produce ideas.

Determine Your Objective

Aim to collect as much relevant data as possible about the content you wish to make before you begin to understand the source. Define what you understand about it by now and what data is still required.

Though it sounds simple, the further you can clearly explain your actual idea, the greater the odds of producing practical ideas are.

Limits to Keep an Eye Out For.

It can impede imagination to convey that every idea is a valid idea, so ensure the aims are ambitious and precise enough. One approach to get some of the viewers' genuinely innovative thoughts is to set limits.

If the ultimate aim is to cut prices, suggestions such as investing truly little on content would certainly come to mind when you want to save up. The thoughts you get, though, would vary greatly if you ask yourself: "How could I save 50% on expenses and create unique and engaging content?".

Deduction

The goal of creating original approaches is to improve what is already present as well as to produce something new.

From a different angle, coming up with entirely novel solutions will help you tackle your creativity block. It helps you to widen the spectrum of thoughts beyond the present style of learning, which inevitably leads to much more ideas.

Sometimes, creators, influencers, and public figures use current ideas or behavioral templates while attempting to get started on a social media platform instead of attempting to think of the latest ideas. The concern with this technique is that it does not encourage you to pursue multiple options and limits the number of possibilities.

5.5: About Yourself

Who are you?

Create a clip of yourself being introduced. Who are you, what are you doing? On your YouTube channel, Tik Tok, or Instagram profile, what should viewers hope to see? How frequently do you upload photos or videos? Create videos to let them know exactly what they should expect, inviting viewers to your channel or page. Aim to give a convincing argument for audiences to click on the subscribe button on YouTube and follow on Instagram or Tik Tok.

Vlogging

Making Vlogs can be informative, fun, intimate, anything you would like to create of it, much like traditional writing. Almost all influencers and public figures may use material from vlogs to involve fans and expand their communities.

A Day in Your Life

YouTubers love to walk through The Day in your Life videos from another's perspective. Once you wake up the next morning and lead audiences to a normal day in your schedule, start filming.

Matt D'Avella Via YouTube

Behind-the-curtainContent

Showcase to the viewers what's going on at the back end of your Instagram account, YouTube channel, or Tik Tok account. With this famous video style, let your audience see behind the curtains. You can display your room, your house, your workplace, your city, anywhere else you enjoy.

20 Questions

You could make short clips or long clips (depending on your preference or niche) playing a game of 20 questions. These questions can be personal or silly, and the best have a little bit of both. Letting your audience be closer to you is what this accomplishes.

'Draw My Life.'

These kinds of videos are often found on YouTube, where the creator essentially draws their life often on a whiteboard with stick figures and narrating their life so far. Of course, you decide how much or how little you wish to say about yourself. Majority 'Draw my life' videos include key events or milestones in their lives.

You can even introduce your family, background, and friends in these.

5.6: Trending Content Ideas

Teach them How to Cook (or how not to)

This kind of content is often made by entertainment-focused or cooking influencers. You can make it an A grade cooking tutorial, or you could completely twist it depending on your creativity and teach people how not to cook but let them have an enjoyable time watching creators do it wrong.

For example, YouTuber 'Simply Nailogical' made a video called 'Baking a cake with Nail Polish' on 18th September 2016, which got over 5 Million views. The cake was quite inedible but still entertaining to watch to over 5 Million people.

You can make this an Instagram post, a Tik-Tok video, or a YouTube video.

Workout Routine

As it's time to start working out, lots of folks look towards YouTube videos, quick Tik Tok hacks, or Instagram posts/IGTV videos for specific fitness routines, as well as how to do those workouts. Both common subjects are exercise, stretching, or shape footage.

Understanding the Complicated Mess

Informative and aurally captivating means of presenting data and figures that could otherwise be dull or difficult to grasp is infographics related content. Content that helps your audience's day a little easier. Every genre of content has specific things that not everyone understands, so try finding the most commonly found problem in yours and present content on that!

Reviewing other People's Products

One of the most common kinds of information on these social media platforms is product reviews. Before deciding to buy, thousands of viewers check out this insightful content. Tech gadgets and make-up items are common themes, but reviews can be sought for all types of goods.

For example, YouTuber Marques Brownlee's Niche is tech gadgets, and a majority, maybe even all, of his video's reviews on really expensive gadgets so often people who think about buying a new phone or the PS5 watch his videos to see his opinion on it. His video called 'PlayStation 5 Review: NextGen Gaming!' received almost 6 Million views!

You can make review videos on any and every genre of content! Games, movies, books, food, universities, perfumes, songs, shows, even countries! So, search for things you can review in your niche.

Comedy Videos

In the event that you need to turn into a web sensation, an entertaining video may very well assist you with getting there. A sizable number of the most mainstream recordings on YouTube, Instagram, and Tik Tok ended up in such a state since this sort of content made watchers chuckle or laugh.

Pranks

Viewers love watching tricks. Pull a trick on somebody (innocuous tricks, please) and share the outcomes on your social media platforms.

Tricks have not been altogether contemplated; however, scientists have discovered that individuals find being deceived an extremely aversive encounter. Trick based humor can be coldblooded or kind, cherished or detested; however, it's not straightforward.

Furry Creatures Content

Dogs, little cats, child elephants, the Internet loves charming/interesting creature recordings are considerably more popular than recordings of human children. So, if you have a pet, share it with the world! Everyone loves animals.

Music Videos

Singing a song cover, and original, or even lip-syncing is always a fun sight to see. Indeed, even late-night TV gets in on the good times. Pick a mainstream tune and give it a shot!

If you have a bad voice, don't worry; try making it hilarious by a funny parody where you impress the audience with clever and witty lyrics rather than your vocals.

Fact Check

What are some myths that are commonly believed by the vast majority regarding your niche? Compile all the misconceptions and make a post or video on the matter. Show emotion and teach your audience the stereotypes believed about your niche by the public.

As the internet is filled with so much information, a fair share of it is fake news, so spreading awareness about it would be intriguing for your audience (as long as you stay on topic).

Often people are found spreading rumors without even knowing they are rumors and not facts, so content that addresses the rumors is an interesting concept for anyone.

Needless to say, double-check whether the information you are giving your audience is proven with evidence to be right. Or else those mistakes can decrease your followers/subscribers quick.

Write a catchy caption or thumbnail with a question that quickly catches their interest. For example, '10 Myths you probably believed about professional cooks' or '6 reasons why you should not believe every thing you're told'.

Speed-run

Can you play games as fast as humanely possible?Finish your make-up in under 2 minutes? Or maybe you can make a 3-course meal in under an hour? Show off those skills on social media!

Speed-runs are commonly found on gaming channels so viewers can quickly experience a gameplay without having to play it themselves due to the cost of the game or less time of time.

Time-slip

@jonnajinton Via Instagram on April 17th , 2020

Time-lapse is a method where the casings of the video are caught at a far slower speed than expected. Traffic, mists, and the sunrise all will, in general, be well-known time-slip by subjects. The outcome is frequently hypnotizing.

Some creators make time-lapses of their artwork to show progress quickly as an art piece can take at least a few hours.

Shopping/Mail Hauls

This type of video is particularly well known with style vloggers and beauty. After an outing to the shopping center, flaunt your take piece by piece. From the freshest iPhone to an in-vogue membership box or the most trending toy, individuals love to watch others open boxes. So next time you do another package, don't simply tear into it; make sure you are recording first!

You could even give out your address and your audience would send you mail. Often YouTubers make mail opening videos reviewing all the heartfelt gifts their watchers send them.

Go Live

Why trust that the recap will show individuals what's happened? Take your watchers to the occasion with you by live-streaming to your Instagram Live, Tik Tok Live, or YouTube Live. Even after the session is over, the stream would still be accessible online.

You can schedule a certain day for every week in which you go live and make sure you let everyone know through all your social media platforms, so they are aware and wait for you to go live.

What Most Do

A substantial number of the top Instagrammersare singers, sports brands, actors, footballers, models, and ofcourse, Instagram themselves.The most famous YouTuber channels are often among the genre oftrailer channels, singers, gamers, kids show, hack tutorial channels, and so on.Tik Tokers are often found to be comedians, musicians, artists,etc.

The best content? Ones that are so good that people feel the need to see it on other platforms too, Tik Tok video compilations on YouTube, and Tik Tok videos on Instagram, Live videos on Instagram recorded and put-onYouTube. The type of content that is put across various platforms are the ones that have gone viral or loved enough that users wish to see it almost everywhere.

Conclusion

First things first, it would be beneficial if you ask yourself, what do you have to offer? Why would people want to watch your videos? What are they getting out of the time they spent on your video?

Is it educational? Hilarious? Scary? Relaxing? Silly?Helpful? Inspiring or motivational? Perhaps very random, either way, would your target audience enjoy or show any interest in it?

Maintain originality- the charm of social media is that you can express your thoughts and add a little more to *you*, so to speak. You can grow on YouTube, Tik Tok, and Instagram, only if you have something no one else has to give out. The basic rule to starting a business, 'what's so special about you?' or 'what do you have that no one else does?'. Write down all that comes to mind when answering these questions.

You can not copy peoples' ideas, only your own significant expression of those ideas into your videos, posts, stories, etc.However, if your content seems to be matching someone else's a little too much, change it up, brainstorm a little about what you could do to make it unique, and choose the best one. And be certain you aren't tuning out any other possibilities due to your fears.

Honesty- be honest about your opinions and where you stand. This can be a random video about car reviews or your opinion on white supremacy; it need not matter. Maybe you feel like changing your genre after a long time, but you're afraid of losing the number of followers/subscribers you've gotten so far. Your fear is valid, but you can't force yourself to put out content on something you have no more interest in anymore because you followers/subscriber will notice eventually, and they'll just fade out on their own. So, try being honest, raw, and authentic from the start.

However, being honest does not amount to being insensitive. You're trying to be the person people look up to or look forward to viewing when they're having a difficult day, so try to fill those expectations without disregarding your bad days, of course. Ending things on a positive note and be accepting of the honest truth your followers/subscribers/viewers offer in return.

Humility- Try not to overthink each comment they make because what seems like an hour of thought to you was probably not more than five minutes to them. When you start noticing your growth, don't become egotistic about it, or the people that put you where you are today will leave as fast as they came. Nobody likes a showoff.

Setting boundaries- deciding where you draw the line between your public and personal life is vital. You don't need to broadcast every minute detail about your personal life to the entire world, and you need to value the privacy of the people close to you if you wish for the same.

Motivation- find that mechanism that triggers, leads, and retains your aiming habits. Whether it be intrinsic or extrinsic motivation, keep a daily reminder for it, so you keep that drive and motivation to continue working hard. Grabbing a coffee, chocolate bar, reading, or some inspirational quote is what puts you in a nice mood and sparks wisdom, do it every day.

The physical, internal, cultural, and mental factors which trigger action are involved in motivation. Introjected motivation is when you are driven to work out of the guilt of procrastination or laziness. Identified motivation is when you know you have got work to do, yet you haven't determined anything in regard to it. Try to avoid introjected and identified motivation as it originates from a negative space.

Don't give up if you feel like you are not getting enough growth, stay consistent and keep at it no matter what. If you still feel like there has been no effect, try going over the points again and make sure you keep track of how you have been doing by statistically analyzing yourself.

Soon enough, you will catch yourself with 10,000 followers/subscribers on YouTube, Instagram, and Tik Tok. It is more or less a smooth ride from there. Good Luck!

Dropshipping Business Model on a Budget

The Risk-Low E-Com Guide to Create Your Online Store and Generate Profits with less than 47$

By

Lee Green

Table of Contents

Introduction

With very little startup expenses, dropshipping is an innovative business model.

A dropshipping business is where an owner finds a collection of distributors to deliver and offer goods for their website. However, as in an e-commerce business, instead of owning the merchandise, a third party does much of the distribution and logistics for them. That third party is usually a wholesaler, who on behalf of the business "dropships" the consumer's goods.

When you start a retail shop, there are several factors to consider, but among the most significant aspects, you have to decide whether you'd like to store inventory or have a wholesale distributor. You must purchase goods in bulk, stock, unpack and send them to customers of your products if you want to store inventory. You may, therefore, contract the phase of storing, packaging and exporting to a drop-ship supplier by picking a wholesale distributor. As direct fulfillment, a drop-ship supplier is often described, but both definitions may be used to define the same service.

The wholesaler, who usually manufactures the product, delivers the product at the most basic, any time anyone buys a product, and you get a part of the sale for the product marketing.

Unless the client puts an order for it, you don't pay for the thing.

Dropshipping is an internet-based business model that draws novices and experts alike to choose a niche, create a brand, market and earn money, with probably the minimum entry barriers.

Chapter 1. What is Dropshipping?

Dropshipping is a retail model of e-commerce that enables retailers to offer goods without maintaining any physical inventory. The company sells the product to the buyer through dropshipping and sends the purchase order to a third-party seller, who then delivers the order directly on behalf of the retailer to the customer. Dropshipping sellers may not need to spend in any commodity stock, inventory or storage room and do not manage the phase of fulfillment.

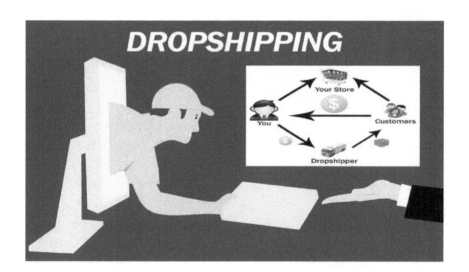

Dropshipping is a form of retail fulfillment, where the goods are ordered from a third-party retailer instead of a store stocks products. The goods are then delivered directly to the customer. This way, the vendor doesn't have to personally manage the product. A familiar sound? Maybe not, but dropshipping is a fulfillment model utilized by 35 percent of online stores.

This is mostly a hands-off process for the store. The retailer doesn't have to buy stock or, in any manner, meet the orders. The third-party retailer, instead, takes control of the product itself.

For startups, dropshipping is great since it does not take as much as the conventional sales model. You don't have to prepare, pay overhead, & stock merchandise in a brick-and-mortar store. Instead, you start an online shop to purchase bulk goods and warehouse space from vendors that already have products.

In dropshipping, the merchant is solely responsible for attracting clients and handling orders, ensuring you'll be a middleman effectively. Despite this, through pricing up the goods you offer, you can gain the lion's share of the profits. It's an easy model of business, so one that can be really successful.

Millions of entrepreneurs switch to dropshipping to get started because it takes less hassle and capital. That's why you're probably interested. And the best of all news? Through dropshipping, you can create a company right from your laptop that is profitable in the long term.

There are several pitfalls and benefits, of course, and it is essential that we check at them before you launch your own e-commerce dropshipping firm. However, once you realize the positives and negatives of dropshipping, it'll be a breeze to learn how to do so effectively.

1.1 Benefits of dropshipping

For aspiring entrepreneurs, dropshipping is a smart business move to start with, which is accessible. You can easily evaluate multiple business concepts with a small downside with dropshipping, which helps you to think a lot about how to pick and sell in-demand goods. Here are a couple more explanations why dropshipping is a popular business.

1. Little capital is required

Perhaps the greatest benefit to dropshipping is that an e-commerce website can be opened without needing to spend thousands of dollars in stock upfront. Typically, retailers have had to bundle up large quantities of inventory with capital investments.

For the dropshipping model, unless you have already made the transaction and have been charged by the consumer, you may not have to buy a product. It is possible to start sourcing goods without substantial up-front inventory investments and launch a profitable dropshipping company with very little capital. And since you are not committed to sales, as in a typical retail sector, there is less chance of launching a dropshipping shop through any inventory bought up front.

2. Easy to get started

It's also simpler to operate an e-commerce company because you don't have to interact with physical products. You don't have to take stress with dropshipping about:

- Paying for a warehouse or managing it

- Tracking inventory for any accounting reasons

- Packing & shipping your orders

- Continually ordering products & managing stock level

- Inbound shipments and handling returns

3. Low overhead

Your overhead expenses are very minimal, and you don't have to deal with buying inventory or maintaining a warehouse. In reality, several popular dropshipping stores are managed as home-based enterprises, needing nothing more to run than a laptop & a few operational expenses. These costs are likely to rise as you expand but are still low relative to standard brick-and-mortar stores.

4. Flexible location

From almost anywhere via an internet connection, a dropshipping company can be managed. You can operate and manage the business as long as you can effectively connect with vendors and consumers.

5. Wide selection of goods to sell

Because you don't really have to pre-purchase any items you market, you can offer your potential clients a variety of trending products. If an item is stored by vendors, you will mark it for sale at no added cost at your online store.

6. Easier for testing

Dropshipping is a valuable form of fulfillment for both the opening of a new store and also for company owners seeking to measure consumers' demand for additional types of items, such as shoes or whole new product ranges. Again, the primary advantage of dropshipping is the opportunity to list and likely sell goods before committing to purchasing a significant quantity of stock.

7. Easier to scale

For a traditional retail firm, you would typically need to perform three times as much work if you get three times the amount of orders. By using dropshipping vendors, suppliers would be liable for more of the work to handle extra orders, helping you to improve with fewer growth pains & little incremental work.

Sales growth can often bring extra work, especially customer service, however companies which use dropshipping scale especially well comparison to standard e-commerce businesses.

8. Dropshipping starts easily.

 In order to get started, you need not be a business guru. You don't really require some past company knowledge, honestly. You will get started easily and learn the rest while you move along if you spend some time to learn its basics.

It is too easy to drop shipping, and it takes so little from you. To help you out, you don't need a warehouse to store goods or a staff. You don't need to think about packaging or storage either. You do not even have to devote a certain period of time in your shop every day. Surprisingly, it's hands-off, especially once you get underway.

All of this means that today you can begin your company. Within a matter of hours, you will begin getting it up and running.

You're going to need some practical skills and the right equipment and tools. You will be equipped with the skills you have to jumpstart your own dropshipping company by the time you've done it.

9. Dropshipping grow easily.

Your business model doesn't even have to alter that much at all when you scale up. As you expand, you'll have to bring more effort into sales and marketing, but your daily life will remain almost the same.

One of the advantages of dropshipping is that when you scale, the costs do not spike. It's convenient to keep rising at a fairly high pace because of this. If you choose to build a little team at any stage, you can manage about anything by yourself, too.

10. Dropshipping doesn't need a big capital.

Since you need very little to start a dropshipping business, you can get underway with minimal funds. Right from your desktop, you can create a whole corporation, and you do not need to make any heavy investment. Your costs would be reasonably low even as your company grows, particularly compared to normal business expenses.

11. Dropshipping is flexible.

This is one of the greatest advantages. You get to be a boss of your own and set your own regulations. It's one of the most versatile occupations anyone can try.

With just a laptop, you can operate from anywhere, and you can operate at the hours that are most comfortable for you. For founders that want a company that fits for them, this is perfect. To get stuff done, you won't have to lean over backward. You choose your own pace instead.

Dropshipping is indeed flexible in that it allows you plenty of space to create choices that fit for you. Whenever you choose, you can quickly list new items, and you can change your plans on the move. You should automate it to work when you're gone, whether you're going on holiday. You get the concept prospects are limitless.

12. Dropshipping manages easily.

Because it doesn't need you to make several commitments, with no hassle, you can manage everything. When you have found and set up suppliers, you are often exclusively liable for your e-commerce store.

Chapter 2. How Dropshipping Works

Dropshipping functions by third-party suppliers, which deliver goods for each order on a just-in-time basis. When a sales order is received by the retailer, they transfer the requirements to the supplier — who manufactures the product.

While dropshipping is used by many e-commerce retailers as the base of their business processes, dropshipping can be used successfully to complement traditional retail inventory-stocking models. Because dropshipping does not create any unused surplus inventory, it may be used for analysis purposes before committing to sale on a marketplace, such as testing the waters.

Dropshipping works because, with the aid of a third party such as a wholesaler or an e-commerce shop, a dropshipper fulfills orders to deliver the goods for an even cheaper price. The majority of dropshippers offer goods directly from Chinese suppliers because the prices of most products in China are very poor. If the wholesaler's price is 5 dollars for a product. A dropshipper sells it for $8 and retains $3 for himself. The bulk of dropshippers target nations with higher purchasing power.

2.1 Awareness about the Supply Chain

You'll see the word "supply chain" a lot in here. It seems like a fancy lingo for the business, but it actually applies to how a product transfers from seller to consumer. We'll use this to explain the method of dropshipping.

2.2 The Supply Chain Process

You, the merchant, are only one puzzle piece. An effective dropshipping mechanism depends on several parties all acting in sync together. The supply chain is just that: producer, supplier, and retailer coordination.

You should split down the supply chain into three simple steps:

- The producer manufactures the goods and supplies them to

   wholesalers & retailers.

Let's say maker A is manufacturing bottles of water. They are marketed in bulk to manufacturers and wholesalers after the bottles come off the assembly line, who switch around & resell the bottles to dealers.

- Suppliers and wholesalers market the products to dealers.

For a particular type of product, a retailer like yourself is searching for a supplier. An arrangement to operate together is then reached between the retailer and the supplier.

A little point here: Although you may order directly from product producers, purchasing from retailers is always much cheaper instead. There are minimum purchasing criteria for most suppliers that can be very high, and you will still have to purchase stock & ship the goods.

So, purchasing directly from the producer might seem quicker, but you would profit more from buying from distributors (dealing with the little profit).

Suppliers are often convenient since all of them are skilled in a specific niche, so the type of items you need can be quickly identified. This also implies that you'll get started to sell super quick.

- Retailers sell goods to buyers.

Suppliers & wholesalers should not market to the public directly; that's the task of the retailer. The last move between the product & the consumer is the supplier.

Online stores from which customers buy goods are provided by retailers. The merchant marks it up again to reach at the final price after the wholesaler rates up the items. By "markup," we apply to fixing a premium that covers the product's cost price and gives you a benefit.

It's that! From start to end, it is the whole supply chain. In business, it's a simple but crucial concept.

You may have noted that no other group has been alluded to as a dropshipper. That is because there is no particular function for "dropshipper." Dropshipping is actually the activity of somebody else delivering goods. Technically, producers, retailers, and merchants will all be dropshippers.

Later on, we'll discuss how to start a retail dropshipping company in this guide. In other terms, you can learn how to become a trader who buys commodities from wholesalers to market to the public. This may indicate that through an online storefront, you sell through eBay or even your own website.

Remember what it's like for the consumer now that you realize what the supply chain is like.

2.3 What is Fulfillment?

Order fulfillment that's all the steps a corporation requires in having a fresh order and bringing the order into the hands of the customer. The procedure includes storing, picking & packaging the products, distributing them and sending the consumer an automatic email to let them know that the product is in transit.

2.4 The Steps to make Order Fulfillment

There are some steps involved in order fulfillment, which are as under:-

1. Receiving inventory.

Essentially, there are two approaches for an eCommerce company to manage inventory. It can decide to receive & stock the in-house inventory, or it can employ an outsourcer for eCommerce order fulfillment to take control of the inventory and other associated activities. The organization would be liable for taking stock, inspecting the product, marking, and maintaining the inventory method if it opts for the first alternative. If the business wishes to outsource or dropships, the order fulfillment agent or supplier can perform certain duties.

2. Storing inventory.

If you plan to stock the inventory yourself, after the receiving portion is finished, there'll be another list of assignments waiting for you. Shelving the inventory and holding a careful watch on what goods come in and what goods are going out would be the key activities on the list so that you can deliver the orders without any complications.

3. Processing the order.

Businesses who outsource order fulfillment do not have to get through the nitty-gritty of order delivery since they actually move on to their partner's order request and let them manage the rest. This is the phase where the order is taken off the shelves, shipped to a packaging station, examined for any damage, packed and transferred to the shipping station for businesses who handle their own product.

4. Shipping the order.

The best delivery strategy is calculated based on the scale, weight and precise specifications of the order. A third-party contractor is typically contracted to complete this phase.

Returns Handling. For online shoppers, the opportunity to refund unwanted goods quickly is a big factor in the purchase phase. You ought to design a crystal straightforward return policy that is readily available to all the customers and workers to ensure the receipt, repair and redemption of the returned goods are as successful as practicable. It will help you prevent needless confusion and errors by making this step automated.

Chapter 3. Whydropshipping is one of the best way to make money in 2021.

According to Forrester (analyst) Reports, the magnitude of online retail revenues would be $370 billion by the end of 2017. In comparison, 23 percent, which amounts to $85.1 billion, would come from dropshipping firms. To many businesses, like startups, this sheer scale alone is attractive.

An online retailer following this concept appears similar to its traditional e-commerce competitors by appearance. Dropshipping may be a well-kept mystery in the e-commerce world as consumers just think about the goods, price and credibility of the shop rather than how the goods are sourced and who delivers the shipments.

In summary,' dropshipping' is a business strategy in which the supplier does not directly hold the inventory or process the orders in his or her control. Both orders are delivered directly from a wholesaler and delivered. This encourages the supplier to concentrate on the business's selling aspect.

Many major e-commerce names, such as Zappos, began with dropshipping. For those that seek motivation, billion-dollar dropshipping internet store Wayfair or the milliondollarBlinds.com are top examples today.

Five explanations of how the dropshipping business strategy appeals to both startups and experienced entrepreneurs are offered below. These issues in traditional e-commerce have been nagging challenges, which can be addressed with the dropshipping model immediately.

3.1 Dropshipping Is The E-Commerce Future

It seem that dropshipping will be the future of e-commerce. Here are some main reasons which explain this concept.

Sourcing of Product:

Conventional e-commerce stores must directly import supplies from wholesalers, frequently based in various countries. They often need goods to be bought in bulk and are then shipped prior to being promoted and distributed to the local warehouse. A lot of time, money & resources are required for the whole phase. The presence of expensive intermediaries, such as banks, freight shipments and export-import brokers, also involves it.

The dropshipping model, however, enables manufacturers to market goods for large quantities of each product without needing to think about sourcing. The entire method is substantially simplified with just a turn-key e-commerce storefront such as Shopify and a dropshipping software like Oberlo. The retailer may choose to notify the distributors via e-mail to tell them that their supplies are now being shipped to the store. The most of the procedure can be quickly handled from the dashboard, such as uploading product images, updating pricing and order monitoring.

Storage

A traditional e-commerce store, particularly as it carries multiple or large products, requires large storage spaces. It might be imaginable to store ten to 100 items, but storing 1,000 or 1,000,000 items will cost a real fortune that is not within the reach of a start-up. This high warehouse rent issue is addressed by the dropshipping model since the goods remain with the distributor or wholesale retailer until they are bought.

Order fulfillment

Many pioneers of e-commerce do not foresee investing most of their time picking, packaging and delivering orders. They should, of course, outsource the order fulfillment for ease to a boutique e-commerce fulfillment, such as ShipMonk. The dropshipping model, however, facilitates hands-free shipment, since the whole packaging and shipping process is in the possession of the wholesaler or distributor.

Cataloging & photography

A conventional e-commerce shop owner has to take professional-quality images of items that may be very pricey, like a decent digital camera, a light panel, lighting and some more. For a dropshipping control software, this issue is fixed, as the "product importing" function allows for instant picture import.

Scalability

Wayfair.com is a major online dropshipping store that holds 10,000 vendors of more than eight million items. Yes, $8 million. By this business model, such huge scalability is made possible.

Because the retailer just has to work on the publicity and customer care aspect, they don't have to think about the warehouse's rent and other operating expenses skyrocketing.

In conclusion, the dropshipping paradigm offers the ability for tiny startups with minimal capital to contend with large and medium online stores comfortably, rendering the field of e-commerce an equal environment for everyone. That being said, plan in the future to see more e-commerce shops adopting this model.

Chapter 4. Niche And Product Selection

You want a business to start, but the thing that holds you down is the market niche that you feel you need to pick. And, honestly, it can be tricky: you might mention all your interests & passions and yet feel like you haven't hit the singular thing that you were expected to do.

Yet, it can trigger paralysis to place some sort of burden on yourself to choose the very right niche.

Certainly, in choosing a suitable niche business, you like to do your careful research, but it's easier to get up and run than to wait around. You will try ideas that way, enter the market earlier, and benefit from the victories and losses. That way, too, you can still take what you have gained from previous attempts, so step on with fresh concepts if the first company does not take off.

4.1 Steps how to search your right niche

Using the following five methods to find your niche, whether you're unable to determine or you need more information to work with.

1. Identify your interests & passions.

This could be something that you have achieved before. But, if you haven't, quickly make a compilation of 10 topical passions and areas of passion.

Business isn't easy, and it can challenge you at any stage. If you work in an area you don't care for, the likelihood of leaving will increase significantly — especially like a first sole proprietor.

This doesn't mean that a better match has to be found. You can stay with it if you are excited about any part of running the business. If you don't care about the issue, you might not be able to easily find the drive to persevere within.

2. Identify problems that you can solve.

You're able to get to narrow down your choices with your list of ten topics in hand. You first need to identify challenges that your target clients are facing to build a viable enterprise, then decide if you can potentially fix them. Here are a few items you should do to find issues in different niches.

3. Research your competition.

There is not always a bad thing in the presence of competition. It can actually show you that you've discovered a market that's lucrative. Although you do have to do an in-depth analysis of competing pages. Build a fresh spreadsheet and start tracking all the competing websites that you can find.

And find out whether there's already an opening in the crowd to stick out. Are you still willing to rate the keywords? Is there really a way to distinguish and build a unique offer for yourself? Here are some indications that you will enter a niche and flourish, even though it is already covered by other sites:

- Content of poor quality. In a niche where several company owners are not delivering high-quality, informative content that suits the viewer, it's easy to outrank the competitors.

- Lack of transparency. By establishing an authentic and accessible identity in a niche where most platforms are faceless and unnecessarily corporate, many internet marketers have disrupted whole industries.

- The lack of paid competitiveness. If you have noticed a keyword with a relatively high search rate but little competition with paying ads, there is undoubtedly a potential for you to upset the business.

4. Determine the profitability of the niche.

You need to have a fairly decent understanding now about what niche you're about to get into. You might not have limited your selection down to a particular region of the topic, but you've certainly noticed a few suggestions that you feel pretty good about. It's important to have an idea at this stage about how much money you have the opportunity to make in your niche. A fine way to go to continue your search is ClickBank.

So, browse the category's best brands. That is not a positive indication if you can't locate any offers. It could mean that the niche could not be monetized by someone.

You're in luck if the quest throws up a good amount of products — just not an excessive amount of products. Take notice of pricing points such that your own goods can be marketed in a fair way.

Bear in mind, though, that you may not have to launch your organization with your own product offering. You should collaborate in your niche with product makers, marketers and site owners to start earning commissions when working on your innovative solution.

5. Test your idea.

You are now prepared with all the knowledge you need to pick a niche, and checking your proposal is the only thing needed to do. Setting up a landing page for pre-sales of a product you're producing is one easy way to do this. Through paying ads, you will then push traffic to this page.

That doesn't actually mean that you are not in a viable niche, even though you don't get pre-sales. Your message may not be quite correct, or you haven't found the right deal yet. You will maximize conversions by using A/B split testing to figure out whether there is something preventing the target group from taking action or not.

You will sell to two fundamental markets: customer and corporation. Such divisions are reasonably clear. "For example, if you sell women's clothes from a department shop, shoppers are your target market; if you sell office supplies, companies are your target market (this is referred to as "B2B" sales). In certain instances, for example, you could be selling to both corporations and people if you operate a printing company.

No company, especially a small one, can be everything to all individuals. The more you can describe your target group broadly, the stronger. For even the larger corporations, this method is recognized as building a market and is crucial to growth. Walmart and Tiffany are also stores, but they have somewhat different niches: Walmart caters to bargain-minded customers, while Tiffany tends to luxury jewelry buyers.

"Some entrepreneurs make the error of slipping into the "all over the map" pit instead of building a niche, believing they can do many things and be successful at all of them. Falkenstein warns that these individuals soon learn a difficult lesson: "Smaller is larger in market, and smaller is not across the map; it is extremely focused."

4.2 Creating a good niche

Keep in mind these important to create a good niche:

1. Make a wish list.

Who do you like to do business with? Be as descriptive as you are capable of. Identify the regional spectrum and the kinds of firms or clients that you want your organization to target. You can't make contact if you do not really know whom you are going to do business with. Falkenstein cautions, "You must recognize that you can't do business with everyone." Otherwise, you risk leaving yourself exhausted and confusing your buyers.

The trend is toward small niches these days. It's not precise enough to target teens; targeting adult, African American teenagers with the family incomes of $40,000 or more is. It is too large to target corporations that market apps; it is a better aim to target Northern California-based firms that offer internet software distribution and training that have sales of $15 million or more.

2. Focus.

Clarify what you intend to sell, knowing that a) to all customers, you can't be all items and b) smaller is better. Your specialty isn't the same as that of sector you are employed in. A retail apparel corporation, for example, is not a niche but a sector. Maternity clothes for corporate mothers" may be a more specific niche."

Using these strategies to assist you in starting this focus process:

- Create a compilation of the greatest activities you do and the talents that are inherent in many of them.

- List your accomplishments.

- Identify the important things of life that you've experienced.

- Look for trends that reflect your personality or approach to addressing issues.

Your niche should emerge from your desires and expertise in a normal way. For instance, if you spent 10 years of working in such a consulting firm and also ten years working for such a small, family-owned company, you may actually have to start a consulting company that specializes in limited, family-owned businesses.

3. Describe the customer's worldview.

A good corporation utilizes what Falkenstein called the Platinum Rule: "Do to the others as they're doing to themselves." You will define their desires or desires as you look at the situation from the viewpoint of your prospective clients. Talking to new clients and recognizing their biggest issues is the perfect approach to achieve this.

4. Synthesize.

Your niche can begin to take shape at this point when the opinions and the desires of the consumer and desire to coalesce to create something different. There are five attributes of a Strong Niche:

- In other terms, it relates to your long-term view and carries you where you like to go.

- Somebody else needs it, consumers in particular.

- It is closely arranged.

- It's one-of-a-kind, "the only city game."

- It evolves, enabling you to build multiple profit centers and yet maintain the core market, thus guaranteeing long-term success.

5. Evaluate.

It is now time to test the product or service proposed against the five requirements in Phase 4. Perhaps you'll notice that more business travel than that you're ready for is needed for niche you had in mind. That indicates that one of the above conditions is not met-it will not carry you where you like to go. Scrap it, and pass on to the next proposal.

6. Test.

Test-market it until you have a balance between the niche and the product. "Give individuals an opportunity to purchase your product or service, not just theoretically, but actually put it out there." By giving samples, such as a complimentary mini-seminar or a preview copy of the newsletter, this can be accomplished. "If you spend enormous sums of cash on the initial trial run, you're possibly doing it wrong," she says. The research shouldn't cost you a bunch of money:

7. Go for it!

It is time for your idea to be implemented. This is the most challenging step for many entrepreneurs. But worry not: if you have done your research, it would be a measured risk to reach the business, not simply a chance.

Chapter 5. How to start dropshipping business in 2021

It's not easy to learn the way to start a dropshipping company, as with any type of business. Nevertheless, it's a perfect first move in the world of business. Without keeping any inventory, you may sell to customers. You do not have to pay upfront for goods. And if you are passionate about your new venture, in the long term, you will create a sustainable source of revenue.

In this complete dropshipping guide, suggest taking the following market and financial moves if you are considering dropshipping.

Others are mandatory from the start, and others are only a smart idea, so it will save you time and stress down the line by coping with them up front.

Dropshipping is a method of order fulfillment that helps shop owners to deliver without stocking any stock directly to buyers. If a consumer orders a commodity from a dropshipping shop, it is delivered directly to them by a third-party retailer. The client pays the selling price that you set, you pay the market price of the vendors, and the rest is benefit. You never need to maintain goods or spend in inventory.

You are responsible for designing a website and your own label, as well as selecting and promoting the items you choose to offer in the dropshipping business strategy. Your corporation is therefore liable for the expense of shipping and for setting rates that result in a reasonable profit margin.

Steps For Starting A Dropshipping Profitable Business

Learn to find high-margin products, introduce them to your business, and easily begin selling them.

1. Commit yourself for starting a dropshipping business

Dropshipping, as in any other business, needs considerable effort and a long-term focus. You're going to be deeply surprised if you're looking for a six-figure benefit from 6 weeks of part-time employment. You would be far less likely to get frustrated and leave by entering the organization with reasonable assumptions regarding the commitment needed and the prospects for benefit.

You'll need to spend heavily when beginning a dropshipping venture, utilizing one of the two following currencies: time or funds.

Investing time in dropshipping business

Our recommended strategy, particularly for the first dropshipping developers, is bootstrapping & investing sweat equity to develop your company. For various factors, we prefer this method over spending a huge amount of money:

- You will understand how the organization works inside out, which, as the enterprise expands and scales, will be crucial for handling others.

- You would know your clients and business personally, helping you to make smarter choices.

- You would be less inclined to waste huge amounts on vanity ventures that are not vital to success.

- You will build some new talents that will enable you a stronger entrepreneur.

Realistically, most persons are not ready to leave their work in order to ramp up their own online shop for six months. It might be a little more complicated, but even though you're already doing a 9-to-5 job, it's surely feasible to get underway with dropshipping, assuming you set reasonable standards for your customers about customer support and delivery times. When you continue to expand, as much as working capital and profitability allow, you will move into working long hours on your company.

Both companies and entrepreneurs are specific, but it is feasible to produce a monthly income stream of $1,000-$2,000 within 12 months of working around 10 to 15 hours per week to develop the firm.

Excited regarding starting a new business but not knowing where to begin? This informative guide will show you how to identify great products with strong sales potential that are newly trendy.

If you have the choice of working long hours on your company, that's the best option to increase your profit prospects and the possibility of good dropshipping. It is particularly beneficial in the early days to concentrate all the energies on publicity when creating traction is essential. It would normally take approximately 12 months of full-time jobs based on our knowledge, with a heavy focus on publicity for a dropshipping firm to replace an annual full-time salary of $50,000.

For a very small payout, it might sound like a lot of work, but bear these two points in mind:

When the dropshipping company is up and going, it would actually require considerably less time than from a 40-hour-per-week work to maintain it. In terms of the reliability and scalability that the dropshipping paradigm offers, much of your expenditure pays off.

You establish more than just a revenue stream when you develop a company. You also build an asset that you will market in the future. Be sure that when looking at the true return, you remember the equity valuation you are accruing, and also the cash flow produced.

Investing money in dropshipping business

By spending a lot of capital, it is feasible to develop and grow a dropshipping company, but we suggest against it. We attempted all methods to growing an enterprise (bootstrapping it ourselves vs. outsourcing the procedure), and while we were in the trenches doing much of the work, we had the most progress.

In the early stages, it is vital to have someone who is profoundly involved in the company's future to construct it from the ground up. You would be at the hands of pricey engineers, developers, and advertisers who will easily eat away whatever money you produce without knowing how your organization operates at any stage. You don't have to do everything it yourself, but at the start of your company, we highly advocate becoming the primary motivating power.

To have your company started and operating, you would, though, require a modest cash reserve in the $1,000 range. For limited administrative costs (like web hosting and dropshipping providers), you may need this and to pay some incorporation fees, which we will cover below.

2. Dropshipping business idea to chose

The second phase in studying how to launch a dropshipping company is to do the market research required. You want to find a niche you are interested in and make choices based on how effective it can be, almost like though you were starting a grocery shop and checking at the numerous sites, rivals, and developments. But the fact is, it's tricky to come up with product concepts to offer.

Niche goods also have a more passionate client base, which, through increasing awareness about the items, will make marketing to unique audiences simpler. A good entry point to begin dropshipping without cash could be health, clothes, makeup goods, appliances, phone accessories, or yoga-related pieces.

Any instances of dropshipping stores in a niche may be:

- Dog bow and ties for dog lovers

- Exercise equipment for fitness

- iPhone cases and cables for iPhone owners

- Camping gear for campers

To try the dropshipping business ideas, you may also use the appropriate techniques:

Google Trends could really help you identify whether, as well as the seasons in which they tend to trend, a product is trending up or down. Notice the search volume is not indicated by Google Patterns. But if you're using it, be sure to use a keyword tool such as Keywords Everywhere to cross-check your data to determine the popularity of the product in search.

3. Do competitor research

You want to check about your competitors so that you know what you're trying to sell in your shop and appreciate the way they operate. Your competitors may have great success hints which can help you develop a better marketing strategy for your dropshipping firm.

Limit your study to only five other dropshipping firms, like one or two major players such as Walmart or Ebay, if your business has a number of competitors (that is a positive thing in dropshipping). It will help you remain centered and prepare your next phase.

4. Choose a dropshipping supplier

Choosing a supplier for dropshipping is a crucial move towards creating a profitable dropshipping business. A dropshipping company does not have any goods to ship to consumers without vendors and would thus cease to operate.

At this stage, you analyzed what goods you want to offer and realize that they can be profitable, and you want to know where to find a provider of dropshipping that provides you with the high-quality service that you need to grow. By linking Oberlo to the online store, eCommerce platforms such as Shopify provide a plug-and-play style alternative to find possible suppliers.

5. Build your ecommerce store

An eCommerce platform such as Shopify is the next what you need to launch a dropshipping business. This is the home where you deliver traffic, offer goods, and payments are processed.

These type of platforms makes the e-commerce website simple to create and launch. It is a complete commerce service that connects you to sell and receive payments in several ways, like online, sell in different currencies, and conveniently manage products.

To use e-commerce websites, you don't need to become a programmer or developer either. They have resources to assist with anything from domain name ideas to logo design, and with the store creator and Payment processing themes, you are quickly able to modify the feel and look of your store.

6. Market your dropshipping store

It's time to talk about promoting your new shop, now that you know to start a dropshipping firm. You may want to bring more work into your marketing and promotional activities while developing the dropshipping business strategy to stick out in your market.

You will invest time working on selling and supporting the company in the following ways, with too many stuff about dropshipping being processed:

• Paid ads (Facebook & Google).

For a Facebook ad, the average cost is about 0.97 cents per click, that's not too bad if you're new to social media advertising. Facebook ads are extensible, goods can perform ok on them, and they click into the desire of people to purchase momentum. You can run Google Shopping Ads and target lengthy keywords that are more likely to be purchased by shoppers. Typically, with Google ads, there is more price competition, but it might be worthy of your time to check it out.

- Influencer marketing.

You may have a low funds for marketing your business as a new dropshipper. Influencer marketing is also an affordable way to target audience because individuals are more likely than traditional advertising to trust influencers. When you go this route, start negotiating an affiliate fee versus a flat rate with the influencer. It's a win-win situation, as every sale they're going to make money off, and the cost is going to be less for you.

- Mobile marketing.

Smartphone marketing is a broad term referring to a company that connects with clients on their mobile phones. You can start with a VIP text club, for example, and encourage website users to sign up for the exclusive promotions & deals. Or provide client support through Messenger in a live chat session with shoppers. You can create automated qualified leads, customer loyalty, and cart abandonment campaigns with a mobile marketing tool such as ManyChat to drive sales and profits for your dropshipping business.

Stay updated on what channels are operating and which are not, as with any profitable online business, especially if you invest money in them like paid ads. You can always adjust your marketing plan to lower costs as well as maximize revenue as you keep growing and improve your business.

7. Analyze your offering

You should start looking at the consequences of your diligent work after you've been promoting and operating your dropshipping company for some time. Any analytics will help you address some critical online shop queries, like:

- Sales

What are my channels with the highest performance? Where am I expected to put more ad dollars? What else are my favorite items for sale? What are my greatest clients?

- Behavior of shoppers

Do citizens buy more on their laptops or cell phones? For each unit, what's the conversion rate?

- Margins of profit

Why are the most profitable pieces and variant SKUs? What do my month-over-month revenue and gross income look like?

To track web traffic over time and optimize your search engine optimization activities, you can even use resources like Google Analytics & Search Console. Plus, you review the results monthly to guarantee that your overall plan succeeds with your business, whether you are utilizing third-party software for your social network or messenger marketing.

You want to build a data-informed analytics framework while building a dropshipping e-commerce store. Remain compatible with what you evaluate over time and calculate the consistency of your store against simple KPIs. This will encourage you to make better choices for your store, so move your small business over time to the next level.

Chapter 6. How To identify Best Suppliers For Your New Dropshipping Business

Dropshipping is a model for eCommerce that is increasingly attractive. That is because launching a dropshipping company is simpler (not to say less expensive) than managing inventory for a traditional digital storefront.

The whole model of drop shipment is focused on the retailer doing its job well and delivering orders timely and effectively. It goes without saying, therefore, that identifying the appropriate supplier is one, if not the most important, and a step towards creating a successful brand. If an order is messed up by your supplier/seller, you and your organization are liable, so the trick is to find someone who adheres to the schedule and is open to discuss any problems

The advantages and disadvantages of dropshipping are well known, but it has become far less obvious that the most significant part of beginning a dropshipping business is choosing the right vendors for your WooCommerce shop. Until now.

6.1 The Importance of Selecting The Right Suppliers

A special model for eCommerce is Dropshipping. To retain their own inventories, conventional online retailers compensate. Those expenses are all but offset by dropshipping, so dropshipping would not need substantial start-up investment.

In the other side, dropshipping suggests that you place the destiny of your eCommerce store in the possession of others.

With the dropshipping system, retailers focus on wholesalers, manufacturers, and dealers who meet the orders of the retailers.

The dropshipping puzzle has several parts, and for the greater image, each component is critical. Among those pieces, one of the most significant is dropshipping suppliers. In reality, the finest dropshippers know that a dropshipping eCommerce store can make or break the efficiency and overall reliability of dropshipping suppliers.

6.2 Finding Your Dropshipping Suppliers

It needs you to partner with manufacturers, wholesalers, & distributors to start a dropshipping business. You want to identify vendors who improve the dropshipping business rather than compromise it.

Research Your Products

You have to figure out what types of things you can sell before you can start finding and working with vendors.

You want to address queries in specific, such as:

- Where does the item come from?

- How long would manufacturing take?

- How is it done?

Are there factors of height or weight which might make fulfillment more complicated or more costly?

The purpose is not expertise; however, you want to get to know the goods so that you can help determine which ones are suitable for dropshipping.

Understand the supply chain and recognize the considerations

You need to get familiar with dropship supply chain after nailing down your goods. In other terms, you should to know how it works for dropshipping.

For dropshipping, the items never really go into the hands of the dealer. Instead, an order is issued by the retailer, and a supplier who manages packing and delivery initiates fulfillment. In this way, the dealer is like the director of a dropshipping company.

You can't sell goods if you don't have reputable vendors, which suggests that you don't have a dropshipping business.

You need to get familiar with dropship supply chain since nailing down your products. In other terms, you need to understand how it functions for dropshipping.

For dropshipping, the items never really go into the hands of the dealer. Instead, an order is issued by the retailer and a supplier who manages packing and delivery initiates fulfilment. In this manner, the retailer is just like the director of a dropshipping company.

You can't sell goods if you don't have reputable suppliers, which suggests that you don't have a dropshipping business.

Search for Dropshipping Wholesalers on Google

You will identify the major vendors for your preferred commodities or product types with a Google search.

When you build a preliminary list, by studying the next few queries, take notice of the various characteristics of dropshipping suppliers.

- What is supplier location?

- Will the retailer link with your WooCommerce shop so that fresh orders are immediately submitted for fulfillment?

- What (if any) is the sum of minimum order (MOQ)?

- What support (e.g., mobile, email, chat, etc.) does the provider offer?

- What kind of range of items does the retailer offer?

Subscribe to Dropshipping Suppliers Directories

And if lots of choices pop up in the Google searches, directories will bring even more options. For a broad selection of items, these repositories comprise of web lists of dropshipping vendors and wholesalers.

You should recognize that some of the finest are premium directories, such as Salehoo and Worldwide Labels, implying they need paying subscriptions. There are a lotof free directories accessible that you can access at no fee, like Wholesale Central. Free directories, though, are occasionally obsolete. Newer vendors do not exist, and suppliers are also listed who are no longer in operation.

Usually, premium directories vary in cost from $20 a month for lifetime access to a few hundred bucks. You can find the expense of a premium directory to be beneficial, with free directories often hit-or-miss. There are also premium directories, like Doba, explicitly customized for dropshipping.

Figure Out Your Competitor's Suppliers

It follows that you must see what your competitors do if you want to be successful in the dropshipping field. Do any acknowledgment, in fact, to see which manufacturers are meeting their requirements.

There are a lot of methods to do this, but testing the markets that the competitors sell is the best.

If the supplier is not listed on the page, by making your own order, you will always show the supplier. Since the retailer is pleased, an invoice or packaging slip from them would possibly be included with the shipment. To ask about a partnership with your own dropshipping company, you can then contact the supplier directly.

Attend Trade Seminars

Trade shows have been considered to be an efficient place for manufacturers to set up and grow their companies. So, if you haven't been to a trade seminar yet, add it to the end of the list of to-do events.

You network with other participants within dropship supply chain, like distributors and dropshipping wholesalers, at trade shows. You get an insider's view on current and future products that you should introduce to your online store. For dropshipping businesses, you even get to "talk shop" face-to-face, which is also the most successful way to do business.

Join Industry Groups and Networks

Trade shows facilitate with locating vendors for dropshipping firms, yet another effective resource is business networks and groups.

The majority of retailers, like the identities of their dropshipping vendors, are not willing to share the secrets of their performance. The individuals who enter business groups, however, want to share, learn, & develop. Through being part of the dropshipping network, you will get valuable insight from industry professionals. Your colleagues, for instance, might recommend better suppliers or alert you about suppliers in order to avoid.

Connect with the Manufacturers

Not all manufacturers supply to consumers directly, although there are those who do. Until picking vendors for your eCommerce dropshipping shop, suggest reaching out to the producers of the goods that you will market.

You have far higher margins when a producer chooses to be the distributor than with a traditional retailer or wholesaler. Manufacturers, on the other hand, frequently impose minimum order amounts that could need bigger orders. You might find yourself with considerable inventory to deal in this situation, which is intended to circumvent dropshipping.

Ask the vendor to recommend vendors for you if a manufacturer won't work with you. A recommendation, after all, indicates that the agreements and commitments between a manufacturer and a supplier is successful. For that cause, it is definitely worth putting suggested vendors on your list of possibilities.

Order Samples

There's no substitution for firsthand knowledge, no matter how many feedback or testimonials you find. This is why ordering samples is the next phase in finding the correct dropshipping suppliers for the business.

Ordering samples teaches you a few key things about a supplier. First one is that you get to know the product's consistency yourself.

The second is that you will see how delivery is done by the retailer, and what shipment packaging seems to if a different vendor is involved, and how long it takes to ship and distribute. Suppliers will execute the requests, so buying samples provides you with an idea of what your clients will feel.

Confirm Contract Terms & Fees

You compiled several options, removed any but the most suitable possibilities, ordered tests to assess certain vendors, and decided on your dropshipping company with the right supplier (or suppliers). Negotiating deal conditions and payments is the last option left to do.

New businesses with unproven consumer bases have fewer bargaining leverage relative to mature companies with established customer bases. When it comes to communicating the margins, this is especially true.

Since dropshipping means that you don't have to hold your inventory, there would be low margins. The bulk of inventory costs and expenditures involved with meeting your orders is borne by your supplier(s). With dropshipping, because prices are smaller, gross margins are often lower than if you stored and delivered orders personally.

With margins generally poor, the fees concerned may be the biggest distinction between vendors. Such suppliers, for instance, charge flat per-order rates that are applied to the overall cost of the goods. Per-order payments typically vary from $2 and $5 to cover delivery and shipping costs (although big or unwieldy goods can require higher fees).

In the end, you want to select the supplier(s) that satisfies your specifications and give contracts of appropriate terms.

Chapter 7. Setting Up Your Dropshipping business On A Budget

The establishment of a dropshipping company as an eCommerce business is a perfect way to earn money. Managing a business without the hassle of product and shipping logistics is the most convincing aspect of a dropshipping store

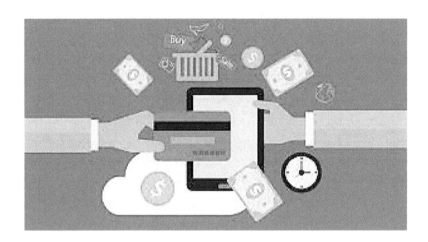

You have already heard stories from businessmen about how costly it is to start a business. This involve accounts of hopelessly pursuing buyers or firms failing because of bleak financials to remain afloat. Do not let this scare you from launching a dropshipping store, as this model enables you to offer low-risk products.

What you need to do is get the orders and call the supplier-the rest is up to them.

There are very few financial barriers associated with the establishment of a dropshipping store when it comes to financing the company. In fact, with around zero initial investment, you can get underway with an online store.

Here's a 7-step feasible plan for launching a dropshipping shop on a budget shoestring.

1. Research Your Options

You'll need to do some research before beginning some form of business.

It requires getting online and finding out the competitors that offer related goods. To see just what each has to suggest, you'll also want to spend a little time investigating the future vendors and distributors.

Each shipping group will have a specific way of doing stuff and pricing models, therefore pay careful attention to those specifics so that you can ensure that you team up with your dropshipping store with the right party.

2. Create a Plan to Stick

You'll need to get a solid plan in progress before you can launch your business activities. A budget is used with this. It's important to decide what your budget is, whether you have $100 or $500 to get underway and ensure that you adhere to it. The easiest way to achieve so is to maintain good track of all your spending to guarantee that as you start up your store, you do not go over the budget.

3. Find Your Niche

In reality, many believe that it is an impossible task. It may be really challenging to appeal to all. Instead, rather than attempting to market could product under the sun, choose the goods focused on a particular niche.

Select a particular area of the business, such as organic pet food or dog clothes, if you decide that you want to market animal-related items.

When you can refine your attention down, you can have a much higher sales rate, and you are more likely to be noticed when customers are looking for a particular form of a product. Your small shop can get lost in the noise of competitors if your focus is too big.

4. Set Up Your eCommerce website

This is the phase through which you finally launch and set up your site with a dropshipping store.

Three of the most successful eCommerce sites accessible to sellers today are Shopify and Wix. It's quick to get started, as well as its user-friendly interface, also for sellers who are not especially tech-savvy, makes configuration and maintenance easy.

With monthly prices of less than $40, Shopify and Wix are both inexpensive alternatives, making it a perfect way to get off on a budget in the digital marketplace. You may also open a Modalyst store to boost the delivery and streamline the distribution process.

You're able to move on to the next stage after you have set up a simple online storefront that has your products selected.

5. Make Meetings With Your Suppliers

When it comes to choosing which provider to use it for your dropshipping shop, there are lots of decisions out there. Because you've done your homework in phase one already, now is the moment where your decision is formalized. Through entering into a contract with the commodity distributor(s) of your choosing, you will do so. Any of the most successful shipping partners makes it simple to get started, and in no time, unlike having to pay such upfront costs, you will be on your way.

The most relevant issues you are asking your prospective suppliers are:

- Do you keep all products in stock?

- How do you care the returns?

- What is your normal or average processing time?

- In which areas do you ship to? Do international shipping available?

- What kind of support did you offer?

- Is there any limit for orders?

You would have a solid understanding about how your suppliers conduct their company until you meet a supplier who addresses certain questions to your satisfaction. In addition, as a seller dealing for them, you'll realize what you need to do. You're on the path to a successful working partnership at this point.

6. Start Selling

Oh, congratulations. In launching your online store, this is one of most exciting steps. It's time to add your product details to your website and start selling until you have all your arrangements and agreements in order.

If customers are not aware of the products, you will not have enough sales, to begin with. You'll want to waste more time and money on ads if this is the case. By beginning with low-cost advertisements on Instagram and Facebook, or advertising on blogs as well as other websites which have a common audience, you will keep advertising costs reasonably small.

7. Optimize Your Site

You should take some time to customize the website until you have some revenue and knowledge under your belt. You can do all this earlier in the process, but waiting to see what is really working before you start to make changes is often a good idea.

There are a broad variety of customization choices for sites such as Shopify and Modalyst, including templates that change the way your website looks and plugins to can customize how your website works. The primary aim here is to tweak the site in ways that make it smoother for your clients and more organized.

As you've seen, all it takes to set up an online store is a few steps, and most of them don't need any money. You're not lonely if you're excited about being an owner of an eCommerce company just don't have a ton of money to launch with. This is why so many platforms are accessible that make it easier to get started without investing a million in the process.

Making sure that it works and prepare a strategy that you will use to guide you when keeping under your budget by setting up your dropshipping business, no matter how small it might be.

Chapter 8. Mistakes To Avoid When Developing Your Dropshipping Business

In an environment that jumps at the chance to make a business deal quick and convenient, Dropshipping tends to have a no for retailers. It might seem like, now, acquiring the goods and marketing with a bit of savvy are your only worries. Yet, if you wish to hold the company afloat, you should not forget about the client's perspective. True, the boring duties of inventory, order filling, and then ensuring shipping can be passed on.

The dropshipping company, however, does not waste any time thinking about the feelings of your client. How do you assume if your client is going to be satisfied? The buyers are the ones who put the money back. Anything falls out the window if they're not satisfied. You would need to consider the duties and what failures typically trigger it all to backfire in order to completely enjoy the advantages of utilizing dropshipping.

Here are a common mistake that leads to the failure end of your dropshipping business, so you should hold these mistakes in mind all the time.

1. Worrying About Shipping Costs.

While shipping costs might be a doozy, it's never productive to stress. In this area, you will need to decide under which your priorities lie. Shipping prices can vary all over the board, depending on where orders come from. This stress can be relieved by setting a flat rate and generally evens out with time. Not only does this make things easier for you, but it's also simple and easy for customers.

2. Relying Much on Vendors.

By putting much trust in such a vendor, a good number of crises can arise. For example, they may go out of business or increase their rates on you if you only use one vendor. They might run out of the items that you expect them to supply. Where would you be then? This is why there should always be a backup for you. It is smart to write up the contract with your vendors for your own insurance to remain aware of your requirements. This will ensure that everyone involved has agreed to uphold what you demand.

3. Expecting Easy Money.

Dropshipping, as we've already established, offers a degree of ease that can seem to make your work easier. Yet, you can't ignore how critical your product is in marketing and all the competition you're going to face. This involves analysis and the creation of a unique approach that will allow the product more attractive than that of anyone else.

4. Making Order Difficult to Access.

When you assure your consumers a simple and quick procedure, they'll want to see the proofs. Set approximate location-based ship dates and require suppliers to keep you posted on the status of the order so that you can keep the consumer aware. This way, you can track shipments whenever you anticipate them to come longer than expected and easily fix issues.

5. Not Enough Brand Display.

Through dropshipping, it may be hard to guarantee the brand remains to be seen in the customer's overall experience. You may not want people to forget regarding you, so it's important to insert as many locations as possible into your brand. You should have customized packing slips, stickers and custom exterior packaging to hold the name included after delivery. Sending a follow-up thank you message or a survey to remind about of you and prove them you think for their feedback at the same time is also not a bad idea.

6. Return Complications.

If you do not have a system for returns set up, things can get messy very quickly. You and your vendor will have to establish a refund policy to avoid this. Customers are going to wait for their refund expectantly, and being disorganized on that front and will not make them feel good. They may also need guidelines explaining how or where to return the product. Organizing a structure for this will save a good amount of confusion and irritation for both you and the client.

7. Selling Trademarked Products

When most people learn about dropshipping and realize that it is not that complicated to do the process, they picture all the things they might sell and make a quick buck.

Many of these goods are items which have been trademarked by a manufacturer. Selling these goods without the manufacturer's specific consent to be a retail agent will lead you to legal issues. This can not only lead to the end of your online shop, but you can also be held personally responsible.

You should, consequently, look at generic items which you can add to your variety of products for sale. Best still, you should swap in goods with white marks. They are plain goods that are available to those who rebrand them through the manufacturer. You will order and get these items customized to suit the brand and display them.

8. Picking the Wrong Field

Once you have abandoned thoughts of selling any product you come across, by concentrating on one field, you can develop your dropshipping business.

You might, however, select the wrong niche in which to operate. Maybe you should pick a niche that isn't lucrative. This may be that it's out of vogue or it's simply not meant for shopping online.

Therefore, to see what will earn you money, you have to do proper market analysis. "Market research" might sound like a complex process in which only major brands participate.

Simple Google searches will, therefore, show you what individuals are interested in and where they purchase them.

9. Poor Relationship With Suppliers

Your vendors are part of your business; they promise that you have the best goods and that they supply your consumers with them. You can be inclined, though, to consider them as workers and handle them as though they are in the hierarchy on a lower rung.

They're not. They are your friends, without whom it would be effectively dead for your dropshipping business. Therefore, you can establish a better relationship with them.

This will have its benefits. When negotiating costs for commodity stock, a strong partnership will work in your favor.

10. Lowering Price To Extreme Levels

Reducing your prices to knock out your competition is also one of the dropshipping failures to avoid.

This is a logical way for you to rise your dropshipping business, you might think. You could have been no farther from the facts. Very low prices indicate to potential customers that your product may be of poor quality.

11. Poor Website Structure

The progress of your dropshipping company depends on the shopping experience your clients have when they browse your online store.

Thus, you have to make sure everything is convenient for them. However, you could rush through the process of establishing your website due to low barrier for entrance into dropshipping. Many beginners do not have the coding skills required to construct an online store.

In conclusion, the primary interest is the customer's experience. Although inventory management and shipping are not your responsibility, you can also ensure that all is well handled. All of these dropshipping failures can be prevented with adequate preparation and careful management, and the business can better manage.

Chapter 9. Smooth Running tips for Your Dropshipping Business

Well, you've done your research, decided to agree on the right dropship goods and roped in the right possible supplier. All of you are planned to begin dropshipping goods and make the mullah! Setting up the company, though, is typically one thing, but a totally different ball game is to manage it on a day-to-day basis. Even if it's a dropshipping company, there are various facets of running a business that you have to remember as a retailer: marketing, refunds, refunds, repairs, inventory, distribution, customer service, and far more. So dive into all these different aspects of managing a dropshipping business.

So far, when covered a lot of details, it involves everything from the fundamentals of dropshipping to the nuances of finding a niche and managing the business. You should have much of a base by now to begin investigating and establishing your own dropshipping company comfortably.

It's possible to get confused and lose track about what's really necessary, with too much to consider. That's why we've built this list of key elements for success. This are the main "must-do" acts that can make the new company or ruin it. If you can perform these effectively, you would be able to get a bunch of other stuff wrong and yet have a decent probability of success.

1.Add Value

The most important performance element is making a good roadmap on how you will bring value to your clients. In the field of dropshipping, where you can contend with legions of other "me too" stores carrying related items, this is critical for both corporations, but even more so.

With dropshipping, it's reasonable to think you're marketing a product to consumers. Yet good small merchants realize that they are offering insights, ideas and solutions, not just the commodity they deliver. You assume you're an e-commerce seller, but you're in the information industry as well.

If you can't create value by quality data and advice, price is the only thing you're left to contend on. While this has been an effective technique for Walmart, it will not help you grow a successful company for dropshipping.

2.Focus on SEO and marketing

The opportunity to push traffic to the new platform is a near second to providing value as a main key factor. A shortage of traffic to their sites is the #1 concern and annoyance faced by modern e-commerce retailers. So many retailers have been slaving away on the ideal platform for months just to unleash it into a community that has no clue it exists.

For the success of your company, advertising and driving traffic is completely necessary and challenging to outsource well, particularly if you have a limited budget and bootstrap your business. In order to build your own SEO, publicity, outreach and guest posting abilities, you have to consider taking the personal initiative.

Within the first 6 - 12 months, where no one know who you are, this is particularly crucial. You need to devote at least 75 percent of your time on publicity, SEO and traffic development for at least 4 to 6 months after your website launch, which is right, 4 to 6 months. You can start reducing and coast a little on the job you put in until you've built a strong marketing base. But it's difficult, early on, to bring so much emphasis on advertising.

3.Marketing Your Dropshipping Business

Marketing is indeed a subjective field, and that there are a billion strategies which can be used to position your brand successfully whilst driving awareness and sales of your brand. It will even help you root out the remainder of the market if the approach is well planned.

4.Social Media Source

Social networking is one of the most efficient ways to promote, advertise, attract clients and share content, so when social networks are now used for digital marketing, it comes as no surprise. For example, Facebook has more than 1.7 billion active members from diverse walks of life, and it is this diversity that makes it so appealing to online marketers.

One thing to note is that it's important to content. No matter how perfect a platform is or how good the product you are offering is, without high quality content backing it up, it means nothing.

5.Customer Ratings & Reviews

A few bad customer ratings will actually ruin a business in dropshipping business model. Think about it: As you order online from websites like ebay and aliexpress, the quality ranking and what other consumers had to tell about it will be one of the determining purchase variables, too, with decrease delivery. A few positive feedback will also give you an advantage over the competition because that is what will help you convert traffic to your website successfully.

6.Email Marketing

In a digital marketer's pack, this one of the most neglected tools. To keep your clients in the loop for any major changes within company, email marketing may be used: Price increases, promotions, coupons, content related to the commodity, and content unique to the industry are only some of the forms email marketing may be utilized.

7.Growth Hacking

Growth hacking is a cheap but highly productive way to get online creative marketing campaigns. A few definitions of growth hacking involve retargeting old campaigns and featuring in your own niche as a guest writer for a popular website. Any of this commonly involves content marketing.

Chapter 10. How To Maximize Your Chances Of Success?

There are only a couple more tips you should adopt to maximize the chances of long-term growth if you are willing to take the plunge and attempt dropshipping. Second, that doesn't mean you can approach a dropshipping business because it's risk-free simply because there are no setup costs involved with purchasing and managing goods. You're also spending a lot of time choosing the right dropshippers while designing your website, so consider it as an investment and do careful preliminary research.

1. Things To Remember

What do you want to sell? How profitable is the surroundings? How can you gain clients and distinguish yourself? Inside the same room, is there a smaller niche that is less competitive? When they find a particular market and curate their goods like a pro, most individuals who operate a purely dropshipping model have seen the most growth, ensuring that any last item they offer is a successful match for their niche audience with their brand.

After you develop your list of possible dropshippers, carry out test orders and then watch for the items to arrive, thinking like a consumer. How long can any order take? What is the feeling of unboxing like? What is the commodity standard itself? This will help you distinguish between possible dropshippers or confirm that positive consumer service is offered by the one you want.

Note that the goods themselves may not be the differentiator for your business.

After you have chosen your dropshippers and products, note that the products themselves may not be the differentiator for your business. So ask what else you should count on to make the deal. This is another explanation why test orders are a wonderful idea since they encourage you to obtain the item and explain its functionality and advantages as a client might. In a way which really shows it off, you can even take high-quality, professional pictures of the product. Armed with exclusive explanations of the goods and images that are separate from all the other product photos, you would be able to start standing out.

Your bread and butter is definitely going to be a well-executed campaign strategy, so devote time and money on each section of it, from finding your potential audience to interacting with influencers on social media in your niche. Targeted commercials can be a perfect way to kick start your site to bring your name on the mind of your client base.

When it relates to your return policies, delivery contact and customer support, ensure your ducks are in a line. You'll need to do what you could to serve as the buffer between a dropshipper and your client if something goes wrong somewhere in the process. Understand the typical cost of return for each item so that you will notice whether it is large enough to denote a quality issue. If you suspect a consistency problem, talk to your dropshipper or try a different supplier to your issues.

Eventually, note that dropshipping is not a model of "all or nothing." Many of the more profitable corporations follow a hybrid model, making or shipping in-house some goods and employing dropshippers to fill the gaps. The dropshippers are not the key profit-drivers for these firms but are instead a simple, inexpensive way to provide clients with the "extras" they can enjoy. Before you put it in-house, you can even use dropshipped products for upsells, impulse sales, or to try a new model.

As long as you consider the above tips to ensuring that the one you chose is suitable for your business needs, there is definitely a lot to learn from the streamlining and flexibility of using a dropshipper. You will make your dropshipping store run for you in no time with a little of research, negotiation, and setup!

Conclusion

So that concludes our definitive dropshipping guide. You now learn how to set up to kick start your new dropshipping business if you've made it here. Starting up your own business often involves a certain degree of dedication, effort, and ambition to make things work, much as in every other undertaking in life. It's not only about building the business but also about pushing through and knowing how to manage it on a daily basis.

The greatest feature of dropshipping is that you will practice in real-time by checking your goods and concepts, and all you have to do is drop it from your shop if anything doesn't work. This business concept is indeed a perfect opportunity for conventional business models to try out product concepts. Dropshipping creates a secure place to innovate to see what happens without incurring any substantial damages that will surely give business owners the courage to state that they have a working idea of how the market works. The dropshipping business model is an interesting business model to move into with little initial expense and relatively little risk.

A perfect choice to drop shipping if you are only starting to sell online and would like to test the waters first. It's a great way to start your business, even if the margins are low.

As dropshipping can still get started with little investment, before they build their market image, businessmen can start with that too. Ecommerce sites such as Ebay, Shopify, Alibaba and social networking, such as Instagram, Twitter, Reddit, provide vast expertise in user base and content marketing. It also helps newbies to know about establishing an online store, optimizing conversions, generating traffic and other basics of e-commerce.

That's what you need to learn about beginning a dropshipping. Just note, it's not the hard part to launch your dropshipping store, the real challenge is when you get trapped, and your stuff is not being sold. Do not panic, and keep checking as it happens. You're going to get a product soon that sells well.

The Complete Startup Crash Course

How Digital Entrepreneurs Use Continuous Innovation to Create Radically Successful Businesses and How You Can Copy Them

By

Lee Green

Table of Contents

Introduction

An entrepreneur is a clever fellow who wants to create an enterprise in circumstances of intense complexity. More than often, a company's priorities don't always fit the ways people need or want a service or product. New products and new projects stall at some stage or don't live up to their full potential. It is where the Lean Startup model comes in. The core philosophy behind the Lean Startup model, which is an evolution of astute businessmen's management style, promotes an atmosphere that allows new concepts to thrive while finding ways to reduce waste. Sometimes as challenging as it may be, the only way ahead might be to ditch what you have and start again from scratch. In stagnation or unfavorable economic conditions, we all are advised to do something for less. All of you must be well aware of the idea of having to do a great many things with little money along with reinventing ourselves or our systems to cater to the ever-changing needs of our consumers. Astute entrepreneurs have insight plus know means and strategies of evaluating success.

Additionally, they can determine the next steps of action, find shortcomings, and make commensurate changes to change with the changing circumstances and atmosphere to develop and further innovate. It is generally accepted that hard work and determination, combined with historical predictors, are automatic performance measures. However, the future is uncertain, and the old methods of working are just not applicable. The management of the previous century does not work with the instability of today's economy. Frustrated with conventional strategies and approaches to entrepreneurship, the creative entrepreneurs begin looking for other ideas to bring to the test. They all have come up with the Lean Startup model that focuses on innovation and getting to know customers' needs and habits to create a better product or service. It focuses on the correct process, that is, to work better and not simply harder to solve difficult circumstances. Whether it is a start-up of tech, small businesses, or a project inside a big corporation, Launching a new organization has long beena hit-or-the-miss proposition. According to the decades-old formula, you always write a marketing strategy, pitch this to the investors, build a team, launcha product, & start to sell it as much as you possibly can. &somewhere in the chain of events, you will inevitably suffer fatal failure. Most of the time, the odds aren't in your favor. A recent study by Harvard Business School reveals that 75 percent of all start-ups crash. But lately,the important countervailing factor has arisen, one which can make the task of beginning a business less dangerous. It's a technique called the "leaned start-up,"& it encourages experimentation over the elaborate organizing, customer input over intuition, & iterative designs over conventional "big designs upfront"expansion. While methodology's only a few years old, and its constructs like "minimum viable product"&"pivoting"—have rapidly taken hold in the start-up community, & business schools have already started modifying the curricula to explain them. The lean start-up movement is changing traditional thinking around entrepreneurship. Newest ventures of every sort try to boost the chances of survival by pursuing the ideals of struggling quickly and learning quickly. Despite methods name, some of the greatest payoffs can be earned by the major corporations that embrace it in the long run. This book shall explore in deep as to how digital entrepreneurs utilize continuous creativity to build fundamentally profitable companies and how you can imitate them.

CHAPTER 1: Lean Start-up

lean start-up is a strategy used on behalf of an established business to create new companies or launch a new product.Method of lean start-up advocates the development of products that customers have already shown they want so that as quick as product's launched, a market will already exist. It is in contrast to creating a brand and then hoping the demand would emerge. Developers of Product can measure consumers' interest in a product & determine how the product may need to be clarified by employing lean start-up principles. The process is referred to as validated learning & can be used to prevent unnecessary usage of the resources in the creation & development of products. If innovation is likely to be failed by lean start-ups, it'll fail cheaply and quickly instead of gradually & expensively, thence the word "fail-fast." Lean start-up's example of customers dictating the type of goods that the respective markets deliver, instead of deciding what products they would be provided.

LEAN STARTUP

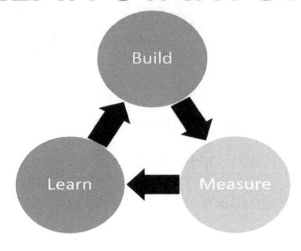

Lean Start-ups vs. the Traditional Businesses

When it comes to hiring, the lean entrepreneurship approach often differentiates itself fromthe conventional company model. Lean start-ups attract employees who can adapt,learn, and work efficiently, whereas conventional firms recruit employees based on knowledge and expertise. Lean start-ups employ multiple financial recording metrics also; they concentrate on the customer acquisition expenses, lifetime consumer value, client churn rate, & how viral the product maybe, instead of relying on revenue statements, balance sheets, and cash flow statements.

Requirements for the Lean Startup

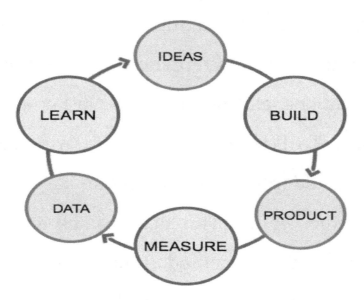

Experimentation is perceived bythe lean start-up approach to be extra valuable than comprehensive planning. A waste of time is viewed as fiveyearsof business plans designed on unknowns, and consumer response is paramount. Instead of the business models, Lean start-ups use business concepts focused on assumptions that are easily checked. Before proceeding, data doesn't have to be completed; it only has to be more than enough. The start-up easily changes to limit the losses & return to the production of goods consumers want when customers do not respond. Failure is generally regarded as the rule. Following this strategy, entrepreneurs validate their theories by engaging with prospective consumers, investors, &partners to evaluate their responses to product specifications, packaging, delivery, and customer retention. With the data, entrepreneurs make tiny changes to goods called iterations, and big adjustments known as pivots fix any major issues. To best suit the current target consumer, this testing process could result in exchanging target customers or altering the product. A problem thatmust be addressed is first defined by the lean start-up method. It then producesthe minimum workable product or smallest product type that enables entrepreneurs to offer prospective buyers. This strategy is simpler and less risky than checking final product production, and decreasing the risk that start-ups facereduces their usual high failure rate. Lean start-ups redefine start-up asan enterprise aiming for scalable growth models, not the one that is determined to follow an established business strategy.

1.1 Learn to build a Lean Start-up

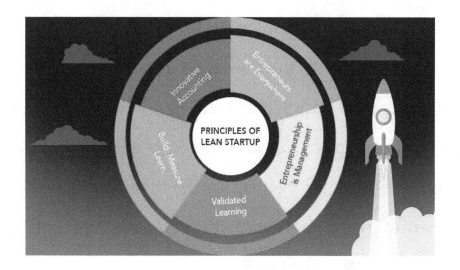

Do you know the 75 percent of all start-ups usually fail? You're likely to encounter obstacles, difficulties, and roadblocks of all sorts, no matter which type of company you're beginning to build. You could spend years on one business idea to fail if you've followed the conventional start-up formula of drafting a business plan, setting up to the investors, developing your product, & selling it. The Lean Startup Methodology is an inexpensive, fast, and less risky technique to carry your business concept to the market. Launching some form of business has always been risky. "Instead of using more traditional methods, the main distinction between building lean start-ups with Lean Start-ups Methodology is thatentrepreneurs must ask themselves that "Should the products be built? "instead of "Can the products be built? It is about identifying a problem, validating the question, and creatinga product that can fix the problem to create a lean start-up. When you create a lean start-up, you need to ensure that your product is consistently checked and verified, so your product's inthe customer's hands as quick as possible. Subsequently, Lean Startups Methodology would help you optimize business growth. To begin creatinga lean start-up, here are three moves entrepreneurs may take: Find, Execute, & Validate it.

Find the Business Idea

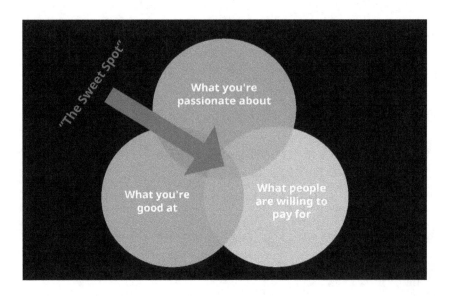

the big question is not: "couldthis be built?" or "Should this be built?" "It puts us in an extraordinary historical moment: the success of collective imaginations depends on our future prosperity. It's important to determine whether the product can fix is significant enough for clients to choose to buy it while selecting a company concept to pursue using the Lean Startup Approach. It can be easy to find a business idea, so it's essential to pay attention to the challenges people face daily. For the product to gain momentum, clients must be aggressively looking for solutions to a problem. It is time to execute the project after you settle ona business idea.

Execute the Business Idea

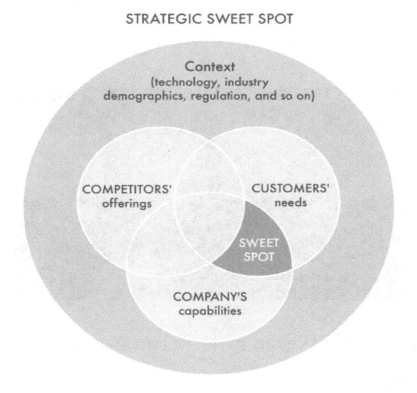

STRATEGIC SWEET SPOT

Next, you can create minimum viable products (MVP). MVP is a version of a product you plan to create, allowingthe team to quickly gather as much knowledge as possible on your prospective consumers and their input on the product. Any Lean Start-up Philosophy advocates recommend that you take the "Kickstarter Approach" for your product, i.e., start selling the product before it's completed to build market value and drive demand in the product while collecting funds for the Lean Startup. It's time to validate the business plan once the business ideasare executed.

Validate the Business idea

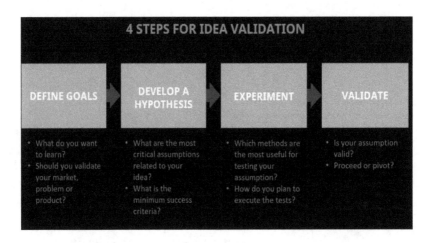

Start-ups do not only exist to make products, make profits, or even support clients.Their main target is to know how to create a profitable enterprise. By conducting multiple trials that allow the entrepreneurs to verify each aspect of the vision, this learning can be scientifically validated. Product validation's a crucial step in the development of profitable Lean Start-ups. In this phase, in the real world, it's time to play with the business idea. Early adopter or otherwise, test the MVP with actual consumers in the industry to see whether the product is feasible and to gain knowledge that you could study. Use this knowledge to determine if you can continue building your product, modifying the product, or pivoting your market plan. If the findings are mainly good from checking MVP in the marketplace, continue to develop your products using your initial approach while integrating tester input. If the outcomes of marketplace MVP research are favorable and unfavorable, tweak the product or business plan to make the product ideally suited to your consumers' desires and needs. If the findings are mainly disappointing from checking MVP in the industry, it's time for pivoting your product & business plan. To adapt vision to suit the desires and the needs of the clients would entail a radical change in your technique and work. Under certain circumstances, mainly unfavorable reviews would indicate that Lean Startup can fully quit the marketplace.

Why should one build a Lean Start-up?

Start-up's different way of seeing atthe growth of innovative and new products, all at the same time highlighting rapid iteration & customer insights, huge vision & great ambition. Buildinga lean start-up is an ideal opportunity for entrepreneurs who need to start an inexpensive company and easily bring them to market. Building lean start-up essentially shortens product creation times and means that developers build products through experimentation & validated learning that satisfy consumer needs.

Example of Lean Startup

For instance, a healthy meal delivery service that targets busy, single twenty-somethings in the urban areas could learn that thirty-something wealthy mothers of newborns in the suburbs have a better market. The business could then alter its delivery schedule & the types of foods it serves to provide new mothers with optimal nutrition. It could also add options for spouses or partners & other children in the household for meals. The lean start-up approach is not intended to be used solely by start-ups. In developing countries where electricity is unreliable, companies such as General Electric have used the technique to develop a new battery for cell phone companies.

CHAPTER 2: Importance of Market Research

The method of evaluating a new product or service's feasibilitythrough surveys carried out directly with prospective consumers is market research. Market analysis helps an organization discover the target market & collect customers' views and the other inputs on product or service participation. This form of research may be performed in-house through the organization itself or a 3rd party company specialising in market analysis. Through polls, product testing, & focus groups, it can be achieved. Usually, research subjects are compensated with the samples of goods or/andpaid nominal stipends for the time. Market analysis isa vital aspect of new products or service's research and development (R&D).

The company uses market testing by engaging individuals with a prospective buyer to test its feasibility or service.

Companies will find out the target customers through market analysis and get customer reviews and input quickly.

This form of research may be performed in-house through the organization itself or an independent company specializing in the market analysis.

The study includes surveys, testing of products, & focus groups.

2.1 Develop an understanding of the Market Research

Figure 2.8 Proper Definition of the Marketing Research Problem

The market research aims to examine the market related to certain products or services to decide how the audience receives them. Itwill include the compilation of information for the market segmentation & product differentiation purposes that could be used to target promotional campaigns and assess what attributes are perceived as a concern by the customer. To complete the process of market analysis, an organization must participate inplenty of activities. Based on the business area being investigated, it needs to collect information. To assess the existence of certain trends or the related data point that it can use indecision-making, the organization needs to evaluate and understand the resulting data. Market research's a vital instrument for helping businesses identify what buyers expect, produce goods that people can use, & maintaina strategic edge over other businesses in their sector.

2.2 Collection of information through Market Research

The market analysis containsa mixture of the primary information, meaning what the organization or a person recruited by a company has collected, & secondary pieces of information, or what outside source has collected.

Primary Information

The Primary data is either compiled by the organization or gathered by an individual or a business contracted to do analysis. Generally speaking, this kind of knowledge falls intotwo categories: exploratory &/or specific research. Exploratory analysis is a less formal choice that works by many open-ended inquiries, resulting in the presentation of questions or challenges that might need to be answered by the enterprise. The relevant study seeks the solutions to questions previously understood that are mostly called to light by exploratory researches.

Secondary Information

Secondary data is data that has already beenobtained from an external agency. Itcould include the demographic statistic from federal census results, research studies by trade groups, or research provided by the other organization working within the same business area.

Example of Market Research

Often firms use market analysis to evaluate potential ideas or gather customer knowledge on what types of products or the services they like and do not have at present. For instance, to test the feasibility of a product or service, a company considering going into the business might perform market research. If consumer interest is confirmed by market research, the company can proceed with the business plan confidently. If not, to make changes to the product to get it inline with consumer expectations, the organization should use market analysis findings.

Components of Market Research

The research of market involves the gathering of information about:

customers – for developing a customer profile

industry & market environment – for understanding factors that are external to the business

competitors – for developingcompetitor profiles.

Learn to research the industry and market environment

the business & market factors analysis will concentrate on knowledge regarding any legal, political, social,economic, and cultural problems or developments that may impact your organization. This external analysis will then be used to obtain knowledge about the composition of the target market, market differences, emerging market patterns, and where the new market prospects may lie. Research on the industry and business outlook could cover:

- Market size & trends
- Business regulations
- Marketing channels
- Market demographics (for example, age, gender, income)
- Sociographic (for example, beliefs & attitudes, lifestyle factors, interests).

Sources that can be used for collecting the data

- Pertinent business & industry associations
- Online trade journal
- Newspapers
- Council businesses support service
- Print media
- Television
- Industry expos along with trade shows

Regional councils &relevant state governmental departments (which is depending upon the industry)

consumer lists or Commercially sold marketing

search engines for Internet

Research the customers

To collect the relevant information about who your clients or future customers are, & what, where, when & how they shop, you can use consumer analysis.

Customer analysis will also provide you with useful insights into your consumers' perceptions towards your organization and your goods and services.

Research on customers may cover:

- Needs & expectations
- Social & lifestyle trends
- Attitude towards you
- Customer demographics (like age, income, gender)
- Attitudes towards your opponents.

Sources for researching customers

- Focus groups
- <u>surveys & questionnaires</u> for staff and customers
- Observations of the customer behavior
- Personal interviews
- Feedbackon points-of-sale
- Sales staff
- Phone surveys
- Social media
- Development offices for local business (local council & independent)

Research the competitors

Your study into competitors will obtain data on current and future competitors. You will use your rival's data to gain knowledge such as the existing business advantages of your competitor, shortcomings in their sales tactics, & how their consumers view their goods and services. Analysis of competitors may cover:

- Present turnover & market shares

- Pricing structures and policies

- Products & services

- Branding, marketing, advertising

Sources for researching competitors

- Competitor marketing & advertising material, the price-lists

- Past clients

- Suppliers

- Official offices like licensing bodies

- Business directories

- Competitor stores, pages on social media,and websites

- Complaints blogs & chat sites

- Competitor print & lists of electronic mailing

- Personal & staff observations

CHAPTER 3: Digital Entrepreneurship

It is important to academic study to consider the conditions and reasons that promote digital entrepreneurship (DE) and to direct market practice and public policies aimed at promoting this development, given its positive impacts on job development and economic growth. Digital entrepreneurship is a concept that determines how entrepreneurship can evolve as digital technology begins to disrupt industry and culture. Digital entrepreneurship illustrates trends in the practice, philosophy, and curriculum of entrepreneurs. In a modern world, digital entrepreneurship encompasses everything new and distinct about entrepreneurship, including:

- New ways of locating customers for entrepreneurial ventures
- Innovative ways of designing and offering products and services
- Unconventional ways of generating revenue and reducing cost
- Identification of fresh opportunities to collaborate with platforms and partners

- New sources of opportunity, risk, and competitive advantage

Digital entrepreneurship opens up new opportunities on a realistic basis for someone dreaming about being an entrepreneur. Some possibilities are more technical, but many others are within reach for someone who learns the fundamental skills of digital entrepreneurship. Such specific skills include looking online for potential clients, prototyping new business concepts, and improving data-based business ideas. Digital entrepreneurship is all about new ways of thinking about entrepreneurship itself and learning new technological skills, which is another way of suggesting that it introduces new entrepreneurship theories. New questions about the policy, chance, and risk are opened up by digital entrepreneurship. Digital entrepreneurship unlocks new opportunities in terms of education to train the future generation of entrepreneurs. 'Doing it' is the perfect way to practice entrepreneurship and draw on the learning. In the normal world, beginning the latest company or releasinga new product is expensive and dangerous for beginners. Not only does the modern world reduce the hurdles to beginning something new, but it provides a range of routes to growth. Educationally, it's such a different environment from case studies, simulations, and business plans. There is also controversy over the precise concept of digital entrepreneurship, partly because it is early and partly because it is changing. What is fresh in digital entrepreneurship can change over time as digital technology progresses. Maybe one day, any business projects will beborn digital,' and digital entrepreneurship will cease to exist as a separate topic. However, today, there is a strong need to help educate entrepreneurs for the modern world and offer a new route to entrepreneurship to more individuals.

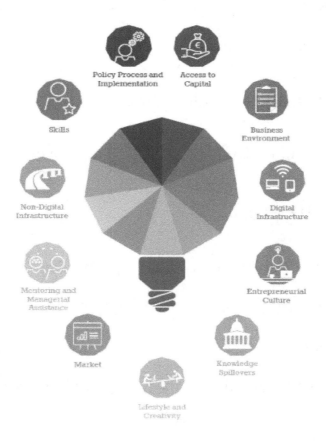

Simple Types of Digital Business Ideas

Digital marketers don't have a good sense of what is possible at the very beginning. It is advised that they begin with one of five basic forms to help beginners conceive of new digital business ideas:

A business offering knowledge on every specialized topic

It is possible to raise revenue through advertising, referrals, sponsorship, or merchandise

A neighborhood enterprise, hosting a vibrant and helpful discussion on every specialized topic

 The sales opportunities are close to the industry of information

An online marketplace that markets goods or services

The objects may be tangible or digital

A matchmaker corporation that puts together two sets of individuals. For instance, a product or service provider (for instance, prospective babysitters) and another group who will need their services are always one group (parents looking for a babysitter). Advertising income is a probability, but with good matches, a transaction fee may also be received.

A promotional organization that draws online clients to a market that already exists

A possible revenue stream here, or advertising, is fees per client referral

An ideal new business plan can be impossible to come up with right from the start, but everyone will easily develop a realistic idea among these five options. As long as they can conceive of a subject that could attract at least a few hundred other individuals, a product or service they want to market, groups of individuals that may support each other, or some small company who could use some promotional assistance, digital entrepreneurs will launch their journey from the beginning. These five basic forms often make it easy for a digital business concept to be shared. In this case, a new business concept is:

A content provider on [your subject]

A [your subject] neighborhood business

An online shop that sells[your product or service]

A matchmaking firm that connects [service providers/group A] to [service users/group B]

The promotion of an online business [a local business]

The options are nearly infinite, and they are still evolving

Digital Entrepreneurship in the face of the Pandemic

Small firms and start-ups have been struck hardest by the recent pandemic than any other area of the economy. To survive a disaster, small firms usually have few resources. Usually, small companies still have little background in the new world of becoming creative, which is now one of their best choices for weathering the storm. In this moment of recession, a variety of digital practices can be considered by small companies. The typical guidance involves applying for federal support, staying in contact with online buyers, and beginning existing products' sales using e-commerce. These are all positive moves, but studies on digital entrepreneurship suggest some additional solutions. For small companies and start-ups, here are three extra fields of digital opportunity.

New models for doing business

It's a smart idea to learn ways to market your current goods online but think about marketing your experience as a new online service. Many families have at least one person with increased time to develop new things or with an immediate need to discover new, more customized ways to entertain themselves. Another option is to offer digital products, such as online classes or digital how-to guides, depending on your expertise. However, digital entrepreneurship helps you pursue brand new areas of operation and offer similar new goods and services. The opportunity to pursue innovative business ideas at little or low cost is a major benefit of digital entrepreneurship. Your new digital company, for instance, may provide useful knowledge that lets customers make other buying choices. During this recession, internet traffic and investment are up and catch these emerging internet traffic sources' attention. Advertisers and marketers are involved and can pay for quality customer leads. Display advertisements, performance advertising, sponsorships, and commission fees from affiliate marketing transactions are new revenue possibilities. Another new potential for digital business is to become a matchmaker, connect individuals who need an online product or service with someone who can better provide it, and charge a purchase fee or percentage. What types of people do you meet already? During this crisis, what are their special needs? And where can you refer them to for assistance? Many of the world's major digital matchmakers, Airbnbs and Ubers, would need to be temporarily replaced by more local alternatives that fit local conditions and will be able to handle local constraints as they evolve.

Perfect the digital business process

An easy way to think about digital business is to see it as an ABC method with three steps: acquisition, behavior, and conversion. The acquisition adds new buyers through social media campaigns, search results, email, search, or social advertisement, among many other platforms to the digital sector. Behavior is what tourists do to fulfill their needs and help them reach their goals through their digital presence. Conversion is the task that each of your guests would like to do, whether it's finishing order, clicking on advertisements, calling for an appointment, or installing a menu. In each of these three critical regions, this problem is an incentive for the organization to develop its capability. Now is a perfect time to create digital marketing campaigns for the acquisition of consumers. When they are ready to buy again, this will make buyers and opportunities ready for it. By enhancing the digital consumer experience, behavior can be changed. To see which ones are more popular, improve interaction, try new features, new content, and new ways to organize and manage your online presence. Your friend, here is the analytics data supplied by your digital company. An integral digital business capability is to turn tourists into future or real customers. Use the time to try new calls to action. It would help if you also used this opportunity to tell clients to do something that would improve their engagement. Practice getting the guests to do easier things such as likes, comments, and shares. Then intensify the participation by signing up for updates and discounts, uploading their material, or scheduling a future appointment. Don't fail to remember how they all come together when you practice each of the digital business ABCs. With promises that can't be met or ambitions that you can't meet, it's easy to have new tourists. Acquire the right visitors who are happy and will convert.

Start experimenting

The freedom to innovate continuously is a key advantage of digital entrepreneurship. There are several fresh ideas to try in each part of the ABC process. Get familiar with the analytics data, which will be from Google Analytics for most digital entrepreneurs. It will provide you with reliable input on what works and what doesn't.

Itis still being practiced by major corporations, conducting hundreds or thousands of tests on their clients every day. If they continue to remain competitive, small firms would need to develop the skills of digital experimentation. Fortunately, the benefit of emerging start-ups is that they can hop on emerging developments that are not yet big enough to interest the big players. A crisis scenario is a hotbed of emerging developments in the quest, new hashtags, new memes, and new points for the conversation to be taken advantage of. Once digital marketers discover innovative business concepts that work with their first 100 to 1,000 visitors, it is fairly inexpensive and easy to scale up such ideas when trends take off. Be on the lookout for new 'nanotrends' as these developments play out, and be ready to expand.

CHAPTER 4: The Best Business

It doesn't need to require a big investment to start a profitable company. You can start a company without spending much capital, or even purchasing inventory, with a great business concept and the right resources. Adapting to a growing economy requires finding new, smart ways to fulfill clients' needs. To find the answer to the following important questions, you have to analyze the market:

What sorts of goods or services will fulfill the new consumer demands?

As an entrepreneur, how can your skills better fulfill those demands?

Any of the money-making, small business ideas that need very little investment are provided below.

4.1 Start your own online Dropshipper business

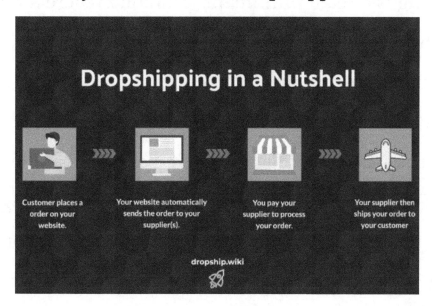

To sell online, you do not need to store inventory or spend a lot of money. You escape the expense of producing goods, handling inventory, and exporting with the dropshipping business by working with third-party vendors that do it all for you.

How it works

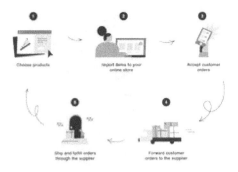

Dropshipping is a retail fulfillment technique where a retailer does not hold the items in storage that it offers. Instead, when a store sells a product using the dropshipping model, it orders the product from a third party and directly sends it to the consumer. As a consequence, the seller doesn't have to handle the items personally. The main contrast between dropshipping and the traditional retail model is that no product is held or controlled by the selling trader. Instead, to execute orders, the seller purchases inventory if appropriate from a third party, typically a wholesaler or retailer. You should start advertising your company using digital marketing tools to drive customers to your site once you're finished setting up your online store, and your site goes live. You'll get an order notice each time they make a transaction. They will complete it after the order is delivered to the supplier. You've just become the manager of your own e-commerce company. To get started with your dropshipping business, link your Wix account with Modalyst or Spocket. You can sell all kinds of great goods at your set prices after procuring products from millions of reliable suppliers. Just try to strike a balance with each sale between competitive prices and how much you earn.

Choose products to sell

You may need to select dropshipping items to sell before you launch your online business. Take the time for clarification of your brand and vision. To figure out what individuals are buying, do some market research. Before selling them in your store, determine the future demand, price, and profit margin of items. For an online shop, you will thrive by finding a way to stand out. Explore specialty items to source and market, and by offering a range, aim to stop placing all the eggs in one bowl. That said, to make your online store easier to browse, aim to organize your items into collections. Keep out of markets that are still saturated with stores. Take the time to set up marketing and advertising efforts to save you time and improve your revenue eventually.

Example: Trending work from home products

Think of what customers do at home to select the right business to establish with little investment. With equipment for living room workouts, open your online fitness shop. Open an adorable store selling puppy items for professionals working from home, such as quiet pet toys. It's all about feeling at ease in your home setting during COVID-19. Itis why items such as sweatshirts, leggings, hoodies, slippers, and socks selling out everywhere. The athleisure trend has a moment. While people do not dress up at home as much, with cute pajama sets or multi-use makeup for a simple beauty routine, they may also look for ways to feel and look healthy. Your customers can also opt for at-the-home beauty items, such as grooming accessories or nail kits, with salons now less available.

As remote employees and students set up shop at home, home office products are also common. You have to dream of tech devices such as lap desks, laptop stands, desk organizers, keyboards, or home storage. The market has also spiked for ergonomic desk chairs that help posture and back alignment or convenient seat cushions. But not all of this is work and no play. As consumers search for new recreation ideas, gaming items have also become popular. As people look for things to do, at-home leisure products, such as game boards, trivia, or knitting equipment, sell well. Shoppers must spend more time cooking at home with restaurants closed. It suggests a spike in sales of kitchenware as well as online food and beverage items. Parents also need childcare and work-life to be tackled. So, consider adding quiet toys and play spaces to your dropshipping company, like the car park mats. Shoppers also like to video chat or watch Netflix with friends without holding their laptops all the time. In the dropshipping shop, try offering bedside mounts and table mounts.

Promote your online store

When you introduce items, it's time for your shop to be advertised. ItIs where a strong approach for e-commerce marketing comes into play. Allow the best of the business software for the e-commerce website. Automate your email marketing promotions and client outreach to save time. Advertise your dropshipping business on Facebook and Instagram with paid campaigns. Work with influencers to support your brands and advertise them to their followers if it's important to your company. In promoting your online dropshipping business, your SEO strategy will also play a crucial role. Itsuggests the development of high-quality advertising and low-budget ads to improve the search engine results' exposure. Increase the visibility of your website with keyword optimization, for example. Let's presume you're selling home clothing for comfortable work. If you include the phrases "luxury comfort wear," "work from home," or "athleisure clothing" in your web copy, when people search for those keywords, you will have a better chance of ranking on Google.

Get creative with branded products designed by you

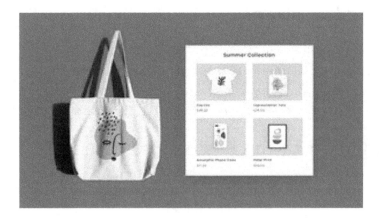

Now, let's take one step further with dropshipping. By linking Printful or Printify to your online shop, you add a personal touch with print on demand. You partner with print-on-demand businesses supplying the inventory, just like with dropshipping. Choose any customizable merchandise and introduce your creative touch, from t-shirts to phone cases, bags, and more. Go ahead and design graphics, quotations, or images to be printed on the chosen items. Start by choosing from thousands of different products to customize your online store and sell your designs. Start a business with funny quotes on a t-shirt. Add photos of your cat to Novelty Socks. Your logo or designs that match your brand create stickers—another cool option: selling goods made by you with original artwork. Yet, to market exclusive designs, you should not have to be a graphic artist. Hire and collaborate with freelance artists to create unique art for your products that are printed on-demand. You will distribute to over 90 places internationally when you receive an order. Forward your orders while managing everything from your Wix dashboard to your chosen supplier. Only think about it; shoppers would rock all over the world your exclusive creations.

Create digital video content

Now that individuals spend more time at home, by taking on new hobbies or returning to old ones, they're looking for ways to keep themselves occupied. Do you work in an industry, such as fitness, restaurants, or education, traditionally requires face-to-face interaction? Use this opportunity to create digital instruction videos, such as cooking demonstrations, workout routines, and more streamed online by people. The shutdown of schools and daycare services in 2021 means that parents have to spend a lot more time with their little ones at home. Moms and dads are searching for ways to keep their children busy, engaged, and learning. So if you are at home and temporarily out of a job, how can you apply your experience to satisfy this market demand? Especially now, family-friendly activities are always trendy. Get ahead of the competition by selling children-friendly video content. Create exercise videos for children if you're a fitness trainer.   Promote the use of child-friendly content, such as workouts or classes for baby yoga. To help parents home-school their children, post daily lessons online. With your children, you can even create an entertaining cooking show. With digital video content, there are distinct pricing models to earn money. To give customers full access to exclusive content, you may charge a monthly channel subscription. You can monetize your content based on the number of viewers if you work with video hosting platforms like YouTube. Selling or renting your videos is another option. Over a 24-48-hour cycle, viewers may download the video or watch it on your site. To give clients an idea of your product and nudge them to make a purchase, consider offering some of your content for free. Zoom, Vimeo, and YouTube can also host live streaming or webinars.

Comprehend the Supply Chain of Dropshipping

Supply chain's some fancy word that defines the journey a commodity takes to move from creation through manufacture and eventually into a customer's hands. If we are talking about suppliers of hard core chains gurus, they would insist that the supply chain stretches all towards mining products to make an object (like oil & rubber). But it's a bit intense. We do not need to be quite so specific. The three most important participants in the dropshipping supply chain must simply be understood: wholesalers,manufacturers, & retailers.

Manufacturers

Manufacturers produce the commodity, & most don't sell directly to the public. They sell bulks to wholesalers & dealers instead. The easiest way to buy goods for resale is to buy straight from the manufacturer, but most of them have minimum purchasing standards you'll desire to follow. When shipping them to consumers, you'll still need to store & re-ship goods. It's also cheaper to buy from the wholesaler for these purposes directly.

Wholesalers

Wholesalers purchase products from manufacturers in bulk, mark them up marginally and then market them to the retailers to sell them to the public. They're normally much smaller than those needed by a vendor if they have buying minimums. Wholesalers normally store goods from thousands of producers, if not a hundred, and prefer to work in a single field or dropshipping niche. Many operators are exclusively wholesalers. Itmeans that they only sell to retailers & not direct to the general public.

Retailers

the retailer is anyone who sells the products directly to the public after adding his margin. If you are running a business that fulfills your orders through dropshipping suppliers, you are a retailer.

Dropshipping is a service, not a role

You will find that "dropshipper" is not one of the supply chain players.Each of the three will operate as drop shippers - manufacturer, wholesaler, and retailer. If the manufacturer is prepared to supply its supplies directly to your consumer, it's "dropshipping" for your sake. Similarly, a supermarket retailer will offer dropship, but its price would not be as favorable as a wholesaler because the manufacturer does not buy it directly. It doesn't mean you're having bulk rates simply because someone declares to bea "dropshipper." It means that, for your sake, the company would ship goods. You desire to ensure that you deal exclusively with a reputable manufacturer or wholesaler to get the best prices.

The order process

Let us observe how the dropshipped order is processed so that you have understood the players involved. We would follow the order put with a theoretical shop, an online seller Phone Outlet, specializing in smartphone accessories, to demonstrate. Phone Outlet dropships all its items directly from the wholesaler that we will call Wholesale Accessories. Here's a sample of what the whole ordering process could look like:

Customer Places Order With Phone Outlet

Allen requires a case for the new smartphone and places an order through the Phone Outlet online store. A few things happen once an order has been approved:

Phone Outlet & Mr. Allen would receive an email of confirmation (likely alike) of new orderswhich store software automatically generates.

During the checkout process, the payment of Mr. Allen is captured and automatically placed into the bank account of Phone Outlet.

Phone Accessory Outlet Places the Order With Its Supplier

The step is generally as artless as sending the confirmation of an email order to a sales representativeat Wholesale Accessories by Phone Outlet. Wholesale Accessories has a credit card from Phone Outlet on file & will charge it for wholesale goods, including handling fees or shipping. Some sophisticated drop shippers will support XML Automatic (a normal format for stock files) orders uploading or the ability to place orders manually online. Still, email is the most common method to placeorders with dropshipping vendors because it is universal & easier to use.

Wholesale accessories ships the order

If items in the stock and wholesaler have positively charged the Phone Outlet card, the order will be boxed up and shipped directly tothe customer by Wholesale Accessories. Although shipments come from the Wholesale Accessories, the name & address of the Phone Outlet would appear on the label of the return address, and the logo would appear on the invoice & packing slip. Wholesale Accessories would then email invoice & tracking numbers to the Phone Outlet once the shipment has been finalized.

Turnaround time is often quicker than you would think on dropshipped orders. In a few hours, most feature suppliers would be capable of gettingthe order outdoor, allowingmerchants to publicize shipping on the same day when they use drop shipping suppliers.

Phone outlet alerts the customer of shipment

When this tracking number's collected, Phone Outlet gives the customer tracking information, potentially using an email interface built into the online store interface. The order and delivery process is complete with the order delivered, the invoice received, and a customer told. The benefit (or loss) of Phone Outlet is the contrast between what this costs Mr. Allen & what this paid for wholesale accessories.

Dropshippers are invisible

The dropshipper is invisible to the end buyer, despite its vital position in the ordering & fulfillment process. Just the Phone Outlet return address & signature would be on the shipment when the package is received. If Mr. Allen obtains the wrong case, he will call Phone Outlet, who would work with Wholesale Accessories behind scenes and get the right item shipped out. To the ultimate buyer, the wholesaler does not exist. Stocking and shipping dropshipping products is the sole responsibility. The merchant is responsible for all else—website creation, marketing, customer support.

4.2 How to Find and Work with Reliable Dropshipping Suppliers

One of the most popular questions ambitious entrepreneurs pose is: What is my e-commerce store's best dropshipping supplier? Supplier directory for dropshipping is a distributor database grouped by niche, market, or commodity. Many of the directories employ a fewscanning mechanisms to ensure that legitimate wholesalers are suppliers listed. Many are managed by for-the profit corporations who charge a fee to use their directories. While membership folders, particularly for brainstorming the ideas, maybe useful, they're by no means essential. If you already knowthe commodity or dropshipping niche that you need to sell, you must locate the big suppliers in the market with a little bit of searching & the techniques mentioned above. Plus, you once startdropshipping company, unless you want to locate suppliers for the other things, you would probably not need to revisit the directory. That said, the supplier directoryis an easy way to scan for or/and browsea vast range of suppliers in 1 location easily and is useful for brainstormingideas for marketing goods or entering niches. If you are short of time and ready to spend cash, a helpful tool may be supplier directories. There isa range of different suppliers and businesses for dropshipping.

Best dropshipping suppliers

CJdropshipping

Oberlo

CROV

DropnShop

Supplymedirect

Modalyst

To make this easier to select best drop shipping companies for specific needs, we will focus on the following factor:

Location and shipping options

So,Where do the supplier's locations exist? How much time is consumed in producing the item afterthe customer has put orders?

Product types

Whichkinds ofproducts they dropship?

Recommended for

And Is the particular suppliers suited for experienced or beginner dropshippers?

Oberlo

Shopify. The Oberlo is dropshipping the platform, making it easier to find AliExpress items to sell in the Shopify store. It is the best online dropshipping supplier directory for Shopify. The platform provides over 30 thirty of the latest dropshipping goods fromvendors across the globe in 60 plus niche categories. Oberlo has free registration, beginning at 29.9 dollars a month for paid plans.

Location & shipping options

In different places around the world, Oberlo links you with suppliers. Usually, each includes many delivery solutions for the clients to send products. On each commodity page in the Oberlo app, you will find what delivery methodsthe supplier uses. thePopular shipping method includes:

China Post. Affordable / Free shipping expenses.Delivery could take 20 to 50 days.

AliExpress Shipping. Affordable costs of shipping. Delivery can take up to 15 days.

ePacket. Affordable / Free shipping expenses. Delivery could take 15 to 30 days.

DHL/UPS/FedEx. Express the shipping expenses. Delivery could take between five to fifteen days.

Product types

So You may find anything that includesbracelets, antiques, car parts, wedding supplies, sunglasses, furniture, and much more.

Recommended for

It's recommended forthe beginner & veteran dropshipper.

CJDropshipping

With fast delivery, it is the best dropshipping service. CJDropshipping is a marketplace that allows retailers to scale up the drop shipping business affordably. You can conveniently import goods directly from 1688 and Taobao marketplaces into the Shopify store, usually at a price lesser than onAliExpress. Along with other dropshipping applications like Oberlo, it's also a free Shopify application that you could add to the store.

Location & shipping options

To perform processing on the same-day for the store, CJDropshipping uses US-based warehouses. UPS, USPS, DHL, & FedEx work with it. The shipping line known as CJPacket will bring goods to the US in 7 to twelve days if you are shipping from China.

Product types

Independent designers &owners of small businesses in China are home to the 1668 and Taobao marketplaces. Via CJDropshipping, there are 100sof millions of listings you may browse, & products vary from mainstream goods to difficult-to-finditems & even the virtual product. If the CJDropshipping app does not have a product, you can uploada request & CJDropshipping wouldlist this once the best source is identified.

Recommended for

The retailer who needs a 1-stop location for all the things drop shipping, including inventory procurement, order preparation, distribution, and fast shipping to United States, is highly recommended.

SupplyMeDirect

It is the strongest dropshipping provider for the UK, US, & European markets for private labels. SupplyMeDirect isa wholesale provider that supports the size of dropshipping business. The app provides private labeling & secure sourcing. It's a free Shopify application that you could contact twenty-four 7, supported by dedicated support staff.

Location & shipping options

The SupplyMeDirect is different. The reason is that nearly 60 percent of the stockresides in the warehousesestablished inthe United States, the UK, Canada, & Europe. It makes shipping reliable and fast. The shipping hasan average time of delivery of 4 to 7 days.

Product types

Any product from apparel to kitchenware, the toys to the accessories, & more

Recommended for

It is best for the dropshippers who intend to sell in the whole world& want fast shipping.

CROV

For the multi-channel vendors, it is the strongest dropshipping provider. CROV links retailers from vetted lists of US vendors to a wide variety of items. It is yet another free-of-cost Shopify app to populate the store with products and automate orders.

Location & shipping options

In the 42 countries, shipping is available. Costs rely on vendors & their shipping processes, which can be found in a directory on every productdetail page. To ship the domestic orders quicker, CROV hasa US warehouse.

Product types

It offers extra than 35 thousand products in more than 20 other trending categories from the selected suppliers.

Recommended for

It is the best for eCommerce sellers. Especially for those who need to sell different products on Amazon, Shopify, & eBay.

Modalyst

It is the greatest supplier of dropshipping high-tickets for US apparel. For online retailers, Modalyst is an automatic dropshipping program. It is known for delivering items that customers would enjoy from the brand names such as DSquare, Calvin Klein, Dolce, and Gabbana, & other famous brands. For any target demographic, Modalyst often features a curated collection of independent & trendy brands. The website hasan official API collaboration withAliExpress Dropshipping, allowing you to access the millions of items with a Google Chrome plugin to connect to your shop with one click.

Location & shipping options

The Modalyst has the own marketplace ofUS manufacturers and products that can offer domestic orders free of charge between six to eight days. Also available are UK dropshipping vendors & Australian dropshippers. Businesses, except countries in South America and Africa, will ship to more than 80 countries in the world

Product types

It generally emphasizes premium and fashionable products. Modalyst is part of the Booster Program of AliExpress also, offering an infinite catalog of items for dropshippers to browse.

Recommended for

It is recommended for users of Shopify who want their shops to add exclusive items. You will also market goods using Modalysts Private Label Software with your branding. You will take advantage of any of the luxury brands and vendors that Modalysts has to sell if you chose the Pro plan.

dropship

It is the best source of dropships for French goods. DropnShop isa dropshipping program for Shopify that provides online sales of French goods. It offers inventory from the top factories of French. It takes the requests from e-commerce partners to diversify product catalog and expand your business due to partnerships with thousands of producers. There'san availability-free plan.

Location & shipping information

To have worldwide delivery at a decent rate, DropnShop partners with numerous suppliers. Every product has different shipping information, but you may find anything you require to know on the product detail page of the app.

Product types

Would you like to sell France's best cosmetics products in your shop? With DropnShop, you may. The supplier also sells 1000s of SKUs, all 100 percent manufactured in France, across several categories, from children's toys to the hair &products of skincare.

Recommended for

It is the best foreCommerce stores. It is best, especially for those whodesire to add the French product to the catalog.

Let us learn to find dropshipping suppliers

Suppliers are not always made equal, like most things inlife. It is also more important to ensure that you are dealing with top-notch players in the dropshipping community. The supplier is a vital part of the dropshipping fulfillment operation.

Before you contact suppliers

Okay, so you've discovered a range of good suppliers & are prepared to go forward—great! Yet you would want to get all ducks ina row before you start approaching businesses.

It would help if you were legal

we discussed earlier, before authorizing you to register for some account, most amazing wholesalers would need confirmation that you are a legal entity. Most wholesalers report their prices to licensed consumers, but you will need to be legally authorized before seeing the type of pricing you will receive. Before contacting vendors, make sure you're lawfully integrated.

Don't be afraid of the phone

One of the strongest worries people have is picking up phone & making the call when it comes to vendors. It is a paralyzing prospect for many. For such problems, you may be capable of sending texts, but you'll have to pick the phone up more frequently than not to get the answers you need. The good news's that this isn't as terrifying as you would imagine. Suppliers, including novice entrepreneurs, are used to having the people calling them. You're going to get someone to answer questions who's polite and happier. Here's a trick to motivate you: just type your questions down in advance. When you have a list of already written questions for asking, it is surprising how easy it's to make the call. Great vendors for dropshipping tends to have most of the following six characteristics:

Expert staff and industry focus

There are knowledgeable distribution agents from top-notch manufacturers who truly know the market and the product lines. It's invaluable to contact a representative with concerns, especially if you're starting a store in a niche you're not too familiar with anything.

Dedicated support representatives

individual sales agent responsible for takinggood care of yourself& any concerns you have should assign you to quality dropshippers. Problems take even longer to fix because we generally must nag the people to take care of a crisis. Getting a single interaction with a supplier allows you to locate the entity responsible for fixing your problems which is very valuable.

Invest in technology

When there are many great suppliers with obsolete websites, suppliers that know the advantages of technology and spend extensively in it are typically a joy to deal with them. For online retailers, features likean inventory of real-time, a detailed online catalog, personalized data feeds & online searchable history of orders are pure pleasure & may help streamline the activities.

Can take orders via email

it may seem like a small challenge, but have to call in each order or put it manually on a website makes handling orders even more time-consuming.

Centrally located

It's helpful to use a centrally placed dropshipper in a big country like the United States since shipments can cover more than 90percent of the country within 2-3 business days. It may take an additional week for shipments to be delivered around the country where a retailer is based on one coast. Centrally placed vendors allow guaranteeing quicker turnaround times reliably, theoretically saving you cash on shipping costs.

Organized and efficient

few vendors have qualified personnel and outstanding processes that contribute to effective and often error-less fulfillment. Every 4th order will be botched by others & make you need to rip the hair out.But without ever using it, it's impossible to tell how a professional supplier is.

While it cannot give youthe full picture, it will give you a better sense of how suppliers perform by placing a few small test orders. You can see:

How to order process is done

How rapidly things ship out

And How fast this follows with monitoring details and invoice

 quality of package when the product arrives

It is important to learn how to distinguish between genuine suppliers of wholesale & retail stores acting as wholesale suppliers when looking for suppliers. A real wholesaler buys straight from the producer & will usually offer you even better prices.

How to spot fake dropshipping companies

You will come acrossa significant number of "fake" wholesalers based on where you're looking. Unfortunately, historically, legal wholesalers are bad at selling and appear to be more difficult to find. It results in non-genuine wholesalers showing more often in searches, usually only intermediaries, so you'll need to be careful.

Following dropshipping tips would help you decide whether it is a legal wholesale supplier.

They want ongoing fees

Real wholesalers don't charge their clients monthly fees for the luxury of doing a business & buying from them. It's usually not legitimate if a retailer asks for a monthly subscription ora service fee. It's necessary to distinguish between the suppliers and directories of suppliers here. Supplier directories are bulk supplier directories grouped by commodity categories or sector & screened to ensure suppliers' authenticity. Many directories, either 1 -time or continuous, can charge a fee, but you do not take it as an indication that the directory itself'sunlawful.

They sell to the public

You would need to register fora wholesale account to get real wholesale rates, demonstrate you are a legal entity, and be accepted before making your first order. So Any wholesale seller selling goods at "wholesale" to the general public is the only retailer offering the items atinflated rates. However, here are a few legal dropshipping charges that you would possibly encounter:

Per-order fees

Depending on the size and complexity of the goods being dispatched, certain dropshippers would chargea dropshipping fee per shipment that can vary from 2-5 dollars or more. As the prices of packaging and delivering individual orderis much greater than shipping bulk order, this is common in the industry.

Minimum order sizes

There would be a minimum beginning order size for certain wholesalers, which is the lowest sum you may have to buy for your 1st order. They perform this to weed out window shopping vendors with questions & minor orders that will not translate into real sales and will waste their resources. If you're dropshipping, some problems may be caused. For starters, what would you might do if you have a minimum order of $500 from a supplier, but your mean order size takes about $100? Only for the privilege of making a dropshipping account do you not want to pre-order $500 of the stuff. It's best to make an offer topay the seller $500 in advance, in this case, to create a loan with them to apply for the dropshipping orders. It helps you fulfill the retailer's minimum purchase obligation (as you are committed to buying a product at least 500 dollars in product) without having to position a single big order without accompanying any customer requests.

Tips for working with dropshipping wholesalers

It's time to start looking for vendors now you can detect a scam from the actual deal! There are a variety of different techniques that you may use, some more successful than others. In order of usefulness and choice, the ways below are enlisted, with the preferred methods enlisted first.

Contact the manufacturer

Itmay be the ideal way for legal bulk vendors to be conveniently identified. Contact the manufacturer to inquire abouttheir wholesale dealers' list if you know the product(s) you intend to dropship. To observe if they dropship and ask about setting an account up, you may then email these wholesalers. Because most wholesalers carry goods from several manufacturers within the niche, you are pursuing, and this strategy would permit you to source a range of items easily. You'll easily be able to find the leading wholesalers in that market after making few calls to leading producers in some niche.

Use Oberlo

Oberlo helps you quickly import goods straight into the Shopify store from vendors and directly send them to your consumers, all in some clicks.

Features

Products can be imported from suppliers

Product customization

Orders are fulfilled automatically

Inventory & price automatic updates

Pricing automation

Search using Google

You may use Google to fetch high-quality suppliers. Itis quite obvious, yet there are somefactors to keep inmind:

You have to search extensively

Wholesales are not good at marketing & promotion. Furthermore, they aren't going to cover the top search results related to"wholesale suppliers for some product X."You will have to do all the research yourself.

Don't judge by their website

Wholesales are now infamous for making '90s-style websites. Although a quality site can suggest a successful supplier in some instances, many legal wholesalers havecringe-worthy website homepages. Don't let you get turned off by the bad design.

Attend a trade show

trade show helps you to engage in a niche with all key manufacturers & wholesalers. It's a perfect method to make friends, all in one place, and research the commodities and suppliers. It only applies if the niche &/or product has already been chosen, and it is not possible for everybody. But it's a perfect method to know vendors and the suppliers in the region if you have the time and resources to participate.

Ways to pay dropshipping suppliers and companies

A large number of suppliers shall accept payments in 1 of 2 ways:

Credit card

Many suppliers will ask you to make the payment by creditcard as you're starting. Paying with creditcards is always the better choice after you've developed a flourishing business. Not only are they easy (no requirement to constantly write checks), but lots of loyalty frequent flier/points miles can be racked up. You will rack up a high number of sales with your creditcard without requiring to pay any real out-of-the-pocket costs when you are purchasing a product for a client who has already paid for it on your website.

Net terms

"Net terms" on invoices are the most typical method to pay the suppliers. Itassumes that you have certain days for paying the retailer with the items you have ordered. So if you're on the "net 30" term, you have exactly 30 days to pay the supplier for the items from the purchase date you ordered by bank draw or check.Usually, before providing net payment terms, a supplier would make you have credit references, so it's lending you money. Itis a normal procedure, but if you have to provide any documentation while paying on net terms, do not be alarmed.

Usually, before providing net payment terms, a supplier would make you have credit references, so it's lending you the money. It's a normal procedure, but if you need to provide any documentation while paying on the net terms, do not be alarmed.Bottom of Form

Top of Form

Bottom of Form

FAQs about dropshipping suppliers

Given below are some of the frequently asked questions, along with answers about the dropshipping suppliers.

How do I find dropshipping suppliers?

On directory vetted such as Oberlo, you can find dropshipping suppliers, colleagues' suggestions, or look the suppliers for the products for brandsyou like. You may also find several excellent alternatives with some research work.

What are the best dropshipping suppliers in 2021?

Some top suppliers for dropshipping are Worldwide Labels, Doba, SaleHoo, AliExpress, Alibaba, Wholesale Central, & CDS.

Is dropshipping still profitable in 2021?

In 2021, dropshipping also represents a viable market opportunity. Since you don't need to spend on the inventory or incur holding expenses, it's a sustainable business model.

Which platform is best for dropshipping?

Combined with the Oberlo, Shopify allows for a streamlined setup for dropshipping. On Oberlo, you can check for vendors and make items available on the branded Shopify website for sale. You make the sales, &your drop shipping supplier will do the rest.

Common questions about dropshipping

We have compiled a list of questions that could be posed by anyone planning to start a new dropshipper business.

How much do I need to invest in starting dropshipping?

While it is difficult to predict exact prices for anyindividual company, to get started, there are few things on which each dropshipping company would need to be spending money. Here's a short rundown of the critical expenditures.

Online store

Estimated price: ~29 dollars per month

To establish & host an online shop, you'll need to find an e-commerce site. We suggest launching a shop at Shopify. You will be capable of syncing source items with Oberlo marketplace conveniently, and you will getaccess to a full range of themes & free branding software so that you can quickly get your company up & running.

Domain name

Estimated price: $5 to 20 per year

Without the domain name, it's difficult to develop trust with clients. Although there isa range of top-leveled domains available (example, example.co example.shop), if one is available, we recommend searching for the .com which suits the brand.

Test orders

Estimated price: Varies

While dropshipping helps you to have limited interference in managing your total product catalog, that you can set aside, also little of the time, cash to test the items you want to sell. You threaten listing products with too many flaws or faults if you don't, which will lead to disappointed consumers anda lot of the time wasted coping with refunds.

Online advertising

Estimated price:the Scales with the business; It is recommended to start budgeting with a minimumof $500

Each e-commerce organization must look for ways of reducing the average cost of acquiring a client across organic networks such as SEO, content marketing, & word of mouth. But advertising is typically an important medium for many product-based firms to start every company. Search engine marketing (the SEM), displays advertising, social media advertising, and smartphone ads are among the most common channels.

How do dropshippers make money?

Dropshipping businesses act like product curators, choosing the best dropshipping products for market to the customers; remember that marketing costs you incur, into both time & money, help the potential customers find, explain, & buy the right products. You will also have to include the cost ofsupporting customers whenever there isa product or ashipping problem. Last butnot least is the original price for whichthe supplier sells a product. With all these prices to be accountable for, the dropshipping business mark up the individual products inexchange for the distribution. It's why the suppliers are okay with having dropshippers markets the products for those people —

dropshipping stores also drive extra sales,whichsupplier would've missed out otherwise. it is good to find out how much this costs to "acquire"customer, & price the products with it in mind.

Is dropshipping a legitimate business?

Dropshipping is essentially a fulfillment model, one used with many global distributors, and is completely legitimate. Satisfying consumer needs and creating brandsthat resonate with the right demographic is also vital for long-term growth, as with any company. Owing to a misconception of howdropshipping works, this question generally occurs. The bulk of discount shops at which you shop are most likely not to sell items they directly make. Dropshipping takes the curated approach & converts it into an online company-fit distribution model. of course, you must do more simple things to operate your business lawfully. To guarantee that you are doing business lawfully in your country, find a lawyer who has specialized in thesematters.

Benefits of dropshipping

For emerging entrepreneurs, dropshipping is a perfect business model to start with because it's accessible. You can easily test multiple business concepts with a small drawback with dropshipping, which helps you learn a lot about picking and selling in-demand goods. In 2021, dropshipping is still a viable market opportunity. Since you don't need to spend in inventory or incur holding expenses, it's a sustainable business model. Combined with Oberlo, Shopify allows for a streamlined setup for dropshipping. On Oberlo, you can check for vendors and make items available on your branded Shopify site for sale. You make purchases, and your drop shipping provider will do the rest.

Less capital is required

Stocking a warehouse takes a lot of money. By using dropshipping, you can eliminate the possibility of falling into debt to start your company. You can launch a dropshipping company with zero inventory instead of buying an extensive inventory and hoping it sells and start making money immediately. Perhaps the greatest bonus of dropshipping is that an e-commerce website can be opened without having to spend thousands of dollars in stock upfront. Traditionally, manufacturers have had to bind up large quantities of inventory with capital investments. For the dropshipping model, unless you have already made the sale and have been paid by the consumer, you do not have to buy a product. It is possible to start sourcing goods without substantial up-front inventory investments and begin a profitable dropshipping company with very little capital. And because you're not dedicated to selling, as in a typical retail company, there's less danger involved in launching a dropshipping shop without any inventory bought upfront.

Easy to get started

Managing an e-commerce business is much easier as you don't have to deal with physical products. With dropshipping, you won't have to worry about:

Warehouse cost and management

Handling returns and inbound shipments

Packing and shipping of your orders

Keeping track of inventory for accounting purposes

Perpetually ordering products

Continuously managing stock level

Low cost of inventory

If you own and warehouse stock, inventory is one of the biggest costs you would have. You can end up with old inventory, causing you to find ways to reduce your inventory, or you may end up with very little inventory, resulting in stockouts and missed sales. Dropshipping lets you escape these challenges and concentrate on increasing your client base and developing your brand.

Low Order Fulfillment Costs

Usually, order fulfillment requires you to store, organize, label, select and carry and ship your inventory. Dropshipping lets all of it be taken care of by a third party. In this arrangement, the sole job is to ensure that they receive customer requests. They will do all the rest.

Low overhead

Your operating rates are minimal because you don't have to do with buying inventory or maintaining a warehouse. In reality, many popular dropshipping stores are managed as home-based enterprises, needing nothing more to run than a laptop and a few recurring costs. These costs are likely to escalate as you expand, but they will still be low relative to those of conventional brick-and-mortar companies.

Flexible location

From just about anywhere with an internet connection, a dropshipping company can be managed. You can run and handle your company as long as you can effectively connect with vendors and clients.

A wide selection of products to sell

Without the limitations of a physical inventory and the associated costs, dropshipping allows you to rapidly, comfortably, and cheaply upgrade your inventory. You will instantly deliver it to your customers without waiting for it to arrive in your factory if you know that a product is doing well for another store or reseller. Without the risk of bringing old products, dropshipping helps you to try new products. You're paying just for what you offer. Since you don't have to pre-purchase the items you sell, you can show your future buyers various trending products. If suppliers store an item, you can list it for sale at no added cost at your online store.

Easier to test

Dropshipping is a valuable form of fulfillment for both the opening of a new store and for company owners looking to measure consumers' demand for additional types of items, such as shoes or whole new product ranges. Again, the primary advantage of dropshipping is the opportunity to list and likely sell goods before committing to purchasing a significant quantity of stock.

Easier to scale

For a typical retail organization, you would typically need to do three times as much work if you get three times the orders. By leveraging dropshipping vendors, suppliers will be responsible for most of the work to handle extra orders, helping you to improve with fewer growing pains and less gradual work. Sales growth can often bring extra labor, especially customer service, but companies that use dropshipping scale particularly well compared to conventional e-commerce companies

Conclusion

Digital entrepreneurship may be clearly described as entrepreneurial businesseswhichare carried through a digital medium. Most studies proved that entrepreneurship a crucial driver for economic development & also for the reduction of unemployment. I's really important to grasp all the principles relevant to entrepreneurship. For meeting market competition & achieve the business target, every entrepreneur must be up to date with changes that arise in the customer's tastes & desires and even in the market. It is often important to use certain new digital technology & softwares to connect with the consumers and increase quality demand. As today's environment is largely dependent on national & global technology, it is important to have thesector's technologies. In this way, digital entrepreneurship plays a critical role in enabling the entrepreneur to conduct all the tasks accurately and efficiently. Using software apps allows any entrepreneur to increase the market demand for his or her product & grow the business both technologically and traditionally. As the Information & communication technologies (ICT) skills are crucial elements of digital enterprise success, it's significant to learn how it allows people to improve their business so that you can use the same for creating your own successful business. Itwill allow any person who engages in the business to learn about digital entrepreneurship in the Present world, changing dramatically in all fields, particularly in information & communication technology (ICT). In this case, the exponential growth of emerging technology with new creative functionalities is changing competitive environment,modifying the general market strategies, systems, and the procedure. For example, on networked economy motorized by new technologies,many businesses or company is becoming tinier with just one person where the partnerships are evolving. Digital Innovative technologies, including big data, social media, and mobile & cloud platforms, are giving rise to new ways of collaborating, exploiting capital, service/product design, creation, anddeployments over the open standards & collaborative technologies. They're, in turn, impacting the market activities through generating job opportunities. Like, Alibaba.com is digital technology that allowed millions of Chinese people to be entrepreneurs. It is also responsible for the creation of employment.

Even digital technologies generate vast job opportunities. They're creating several challenges also.Emerging technologies are modernizing the labor market. Several countries are facing several obstacles, such as Australia, to face economic competition. To face the obstacles and eliminate the barriers, countries are recommended for taking over digital entrepreneurship & achieve an acceptable role. Digital entrepreneurship increases jobs across ICTs like Facebook, social computing, mobile technology, and digital channels. Many firms began digital businesses by selling the products online to meet competition in the industry. As this becomes necessary, focusing on how a business venture must be started is rising with utmost significance. People who need to start a digital company should know the differences betweendigital versus conventional opportunities, downfalls, entrepreneurship, and digital entrepreneurship challenges. The people needa format or digital entrepreneurship system that consists all information about the new digital enterprise, including its features and objectives.

The Golden Ratio Trading Algorithm

Discover the 9+1 Bulletproof Strategies that Helped 113 Dead Broke People Get Out of Debt

By

Andy Magnet

Table of Contents

Introduction:

Defining your corporate plan lets you make the best of your opportunities so you can accomplish your objectives. A successful business plan may be the difference between living and flourishing.

Some companies grow to a stage where the entrepreneur can no longer manage it themselves. Now is a perfect opportunity to start dreaming about a plan that can lead the company to accomplish its goals, e.g. by encouraging people to make choices. Getting a well specified approach to achieve your company goals will also help you clarify your plan to your staff, networks, sponsors, consultants, borrowers, accountants and investors. It's vital for moves like finding finance.

Overall, the effect of a successful plan is that you remain efficient over the long term, stop making typical errors, and stay ahead of the market. A plan provides a common understanding of your goal, making everybody in the company appreciate what you're working for. It will support you:

- Prioritise work

- Make the correct decisions

- Say 'no' to distractions

- Make the best of your place in the marketplace.

When you're experiencing loads of rivalry, developing a plan involves recognizing your benefit and your optimal place in the business. Then you should schedule things to reach you there. In this guide you can find lots of things to focus on so now it's up to you how well you select certain strategies and incorporate them in your business.

Working on a plan will help you discover your keys to progress, and set a course to follow towards reaching your goals. It may also help you grow into new goods or services. Without a consistent business plan, you might make choices that clash with each other, or end up in a bad financial and competitive role.

Chapter 1: Become a YouTuber

Until you even make a video that has viral value (making videos is not incredibly difficult if you enjoy what you do), you have to develop a platform that sticks out. It is also accurate that the videos you produce are the chemical X that will make your channel highlight. However, I have noticed that building a killer channel before releasing the first video is crucial. Let me also figure out that we shall not discuss how to build a channel; what we shall discuss is how to create your channel and make it stand out. Here are the ideas you need to accomplish this:

Create and design your brand

We will not cover, as I have indicated, how to create a channel. I should point out, however, that if you have a Google email and comment account or like YouTube videos, chances are, you already have a channel. It is important to note that your YouTube brand is at the heart of the channel you create. This is what's going to prompt viewers to sign up for your channel. What this means is that the proper attention it deserves must be given to your channel's name. The name of your channel should be memorable and relevant to the content you're going to share with your subscribers and the world. For example, you might create a channel under the name 'beauty within if you want to create how-to-make videos.

If you don't know how to build a channel, here is the link to the portal for creating a channel.

Exude professionalism

You will notice one outstanding thing, which is the quality of video and interactions if you take a second to wade through all the videos that attract many views and comments on YouTube. This simply implies that you have to be professional to create a killer channel and video that draws in millions of views. You need to be skilled in your presentation, how you make the video, and in particular, the technology you use to shoot the video. This means that you can use your iPhone (not recommended) if you do not have a video camera, but make sure to keep the phone as steady as possible. In addition, the audio on your video should be of excellent quality. It also suggests that you should seriously consider adding subtitles to your video if you are not a native

English speaker or have an accent. I can guarantee that your channel will never come close to the status of stardom if your videos are out of focus. Visit some of the more popular channels to find out what is professional by YouTube standards and emulate their video presentation.

Create a video response

Despite the fact that they could generate high-quality sharable material, most YouTubers fail to get their channel noticed. This leaves the uploader with only the possibility that his or her channel may be found by anyone with a broad following. Here's a trick to make sure your channel is out there more easily. The trick is to produce a video answer to a famous video of high quality. In addition, to guarantee that other individuals click through to your platform without actually caring who you are, make your answers either informative or extremely divisive. Video answers that are divisive, fascinating, surprising, or informative can also guarantee you a few subscribers who believe your perspective or design appeals to them. On the other side, even though you don't receive viewers, the chances are good that a couple of your videos would be viewed by anyone who clicks through to your site. Using video responses is a caveat; make sure you do not attempt this trick until there are some really good quality, interesting videos on your channel.

Bait the crowd with reviews

The first thing you probably do anytime you want to purchase an object is to head over to Google to look for ratings. Video analysis is the quickest and more likely to go viral. As long as you make sure that the analysis is thorough and appeals specifically to the crowd of people involved in that specific thing, it really does not matter what gadget or item you review. All of us still search for product feedback (perhaps even you); as such, build a platform that gets many views and subscribers. The endeavor to create a few highly measurable review videos of some famous devices or items is well worth it.

Channel your energy on the channel

If only every three years your favourite musician produced a song, how would that make you feel? The word is Bored! A very similar approach is taken by a YouTube channel. If your commitment to the channel waivers, all the subscribers and subscribers you have gathered will drift off to another channel that consistently offers them videos if it takes you very long to upload. Uploading doesn't stop; you need to be active on the channel, interact with viewers, respond to their comments, and just make sure they feel appreciated and connected to you. If you do seem to keep your audience's interests at heart, they will move on by constantly interacting and uploading videos.

Key point/action step

To develop the mindset and routine necessary for creating an outstanding YouTube channel, fall into the habit of logging onto the site daily, watching a few videos and commenting on those that interest you. This is especially important because it will fuel your idea machinery and push you to create videos that people like.

How to Apply What You've Learned?

 I am aware of the fact that too much information can work against you at times; the same applies to your journey for YouTube stardom. To help you out, I have decided that all we have learned will be summarized into an actionable plan that you can easily follow. Let it get to us.

Fuelling your idea tanks

Draw your ideas on YouTube from other videos that are doing well. I can guarantee you that there are other YouTubers in the field, regardless of which field or category you intend to upload to. Visit their channels, view their videos, and take away the best practices from their videos. Watch how they make their videos, voice-overs, etc., and then find out if you can replicate their style but add a flare of personality.

Viral does not come easy.

It is not easy, as stated earlier, to create viral videos. Sadly, to create viral videos, there is no trick or outright blueprint. There is only one definite way, on the other hand, to ensure that your videos are near perfection and closer to viral, and that is practice. Practice using various cameras, different lighting, and even different angles to create videos. You increase your video creation abilities when you employ this tactic. Make sure you don't look back in simple terms and say, 'I should have shot that angle differently.'

SEO plays a very central role

We looked at the numerous variables leading to the YouTube and Google rankings. Optimizing the video and platform is key to this rating. This suggests that to make the video rank higher, you have to read what you can about keywords and how to use them efficiently. Fortunately, the internet is full of tools you can use for SEO and keywords. You don't even have to use paying keyword queries since Google's free keyword analytics service works best.

Engagements make all the difference.

Through commenting, enjoying, and uploading their footage, you must actively connect with other YouTubers to push traffic to your channel and posts. When you create video responses to widely famous videos, this is particularly successful. In addition, commitment ensures that you have to interact with YouTube regularly by making and sharing videos as much as possible.

CRYPTO-CURRENCY MISTAKES TO AVOID BY LEE GREEN

Chapter 2: Create an Instagram channel

What is Instagram?

According to Wikipedia, Instagram is an online mobile video sharing, social networking, and mobile photo-sharing service that allows different users to take videos and photos and then share them on different social networking platforms like Flickr, Tumblr, Twitter, and Facebook. As you can see from the description, it is a mobile app for smartphones and is available on Windows mobile, iOS and Android.

With the app, you can add captions and filters to your photos, get likes, and increase followers tremendously. You can also follow friends or whoever else you like to get their pictures on your Instagram feed.

If you are awfully talented in taking amazing pictures or want to turn your many followers into customers, there are many ways you can begin to earn money on Instagram.

A brief history of Instagram

Instagram was officially launched around 2010 and three years later became one of the largest and most engaging social networks. It's no wonder why Mark Zuckerberg, the Facebook CEO and founder, bought this photo-sharing app for a whopping amount of 1 billion dollars from its rightful founders (Mike Krieger and Kevin Systrom). Most people thought he was crazy. At the time of purchase, Instagram had only 13 employees had less than 22 million active users and no website. It has since grown so fast to currently have more than 300 million active users, definitely more than Twitter or Pinterest and over 100 employees. In fact, according to recent research, people are spending more time on Instagram than on Twitter or Facebook. It's the fastest growing social platform in the world, and its future is very bright. Just as it has upgraded Facebook's balance sheet, it can upgrade your income. Instagram's social feeds and easy-to-use editing tools make everyone capable of creating and sharing nice edited pictures today. It has empowered people in unexpected ways, even those who don't bare Bieber, Hilton or Kardashian names. You can use it to share your interests, for instance, skateboarding, art, and other experiences, or just share your photos or videos and make money for such a simple effort. Many big companies are now using this platform to reach out to customers worldwide, and their sales have skyrocketed. Companies like Puma are even hiring Instagrammers with massive, profound, and engaging followings at more than $5000 a day to capture photos that display the respective company products.

Key Point

With over 300 million Instagram users, anything is possible. Think of it as a large billboard in a large intersection where over 300 million people frequent, and you will discover that this is an immensely big number of people. So, whatever it is that you might want to do, whether to gain in popularity or to make money, the potential is limitless.

Basic Tips for Making Money on Instagram

Like many people out there are doing, you can turn this so-called hobby to be a money minting cash cow by following the basic guidelines given below;

Build a follower base

Getting people to follow you is the first step to making money with Instagram. Without a very minimum of a few thousand followers, it will be hard for you to convince any brands to sponsor your posts. Even with the over 300 million users, it doesn't mean that being on Instagram automatically qualifies you to have access to this large number of users; you must strive to get a fraction of this number to follow you. Just like any other product, before you start making sales, you need a market, and this is your followers. Here is how:

1) Increase followers; Take all the time you need to expand on the number of your account followers by interacting with your followers and posting unique photos. You will learn more about this in the next chapter of this book.

2) Use hashtags to attract more people. For every photo you take, make sure that it has at least three hashtags that can add to your viewers. The hashtags should speak about the photo but should be broad enough to show up in numerous searches. Don't worry! You will learn more about hashtags later in this book.

Upload quality images

1) Master your craft; the fact of the matter is that if your photos aren't so good, people will not be willing to buy them. This may mean many different things to different people, but you need to take quality pictures if you want to end up selling them.

2) Use different cameras; avoid limiting yourself to your phone's camera. With Instagram, you can upload photos taken using other devices; all you need is to transfer them to your phone first.

Get yourself a nice camera and notice the significant difference in the quality of photos you take.

Set Up Your Store

Without an online store, you are almost doomed. You can't sell your photos via Instagram directly, so you have to set up an alternative way that people can buy your pictures. Here are some ways you can go about this.

1) Hire a store service; you can sell your photos directly through Services like Twenty20 and soon through their site. You get 20% of the sale, and they handle the printing and shipping for you.

If you want to avoid dealing with printing and shipping orders, this can be useful.

2) Get your own store; you can use your personal website to set up your own online store. You will definitely get more money than you would if you used a hired service, although you will have to take care of orders, as well as shipping and printing the images. For each image you upload to sell on Instagram, it should have a caption containing a link to its store page regardless of which method you use to set up your storefront. So that the link doesn't take up the whole caption space, use Tiny URL or Bit.ly to shorten the address. Take advantage of apps such as 'Hash Bag,' which automatically identifies and posts any items that have the hashtag '#forsale' on your Instagram account to their respective market.

Market your Products

After you gain followers and therefore in a good position to approach and convince any company, do this:

1) Contact companies; you need to explain and convince your target companies how you can help increase awareness for their brand through your Instagram account. Show them how often you update your Instagram feed and give details on the number of followers you have. Carry some sample shots to display and illustrate you know how to take clear, artistic pictures which can shed some positiveness to their product. Services such as Popular Pays and QuickShouts can connect you with companies, which hire aspiring Instagram marketers.

2) Work out a contract. You need to have a clear written contract indicating matters such as the expected number of pictures you are supposed to take and bonuses for the improved number of followers, if any. To protect yourself from being underpaid by the company you are marketing for, sign a contract.

3) Take quality pictures of the service or product. For sure, you wouldn't like to upload a mediocre or bad photo of a product you

are supposed to be marketing. For you to keep the contracts coming in the future, you need to play your role as an ambassador for a given product effectively and uphold the expected standards.

You are free to add some personal touches to the photo, and in fact, you should. You don't want your followers to feel as if this is just one of those advertisements they would spam so easily if they weren't following you. Your followers need to relate to your image on a personal level.

Turn your many followers into Customers

1) Point followers to your blog or site; you should have a link to your company's or personal website or blog always on your Instagram profile. As you continue to gain more random viewers or followers, traffic to your site will also increase. Emphasize your skills. You can showcase your abilities and talents on Instagram, including fashion, web development, photography, and several other fields. Update your current projects and latest work on your Instagram feed always. Remember to use hashtags to attract potential buyers to your image.

2) Take your product's photos. If you run a business that deals with physical items like vehicles, cupcakes or whatever, one of the best ways to advertise your merchandise to new people are through Instagram. Take photos of some of your latest products, then make sure you use hashtags to entice more followers. Some hashtag examples include the product name and use, your company name or slogan. If you have a store page, make sure you link to the product's image comments. Remember to submit the nicest photos you got of the product and avoid those low-quality cameras at all costs.

Offer Brand Takeovers

You can earn some good money by doing an "Instagram takeover" as a substitute for sharing sponsored posts on your own account. It's exactly what it sounds like and is all about posting photos on another person's Instagram account. Either you can get temporary access to the person's or company's account, or you can be asked to supply photos, additional descriptions and hashtags to them. This works especially well for travel accounts, "We supply 5-7 amazing images to a company or tourism board and they feature our photos showcasing how we see the destination," says Bouskill, an Instagrammer.

Sell Your Account

You can sell your account for profit once you have a tremendously successful account. You can even get a six-digit for selling accounts that have 500,000 to a million followers.

Key point

Stay active on Instagram to get as many followers as you can, upload quality images of what you are selling, set up an online store, market your great skills to companies, and then turn your devoted followers to customers. Do "brand take over" or sell your account if you please. Don't forget to put the links and the hashtags on your Instagram images or comments. When you do that, you can watch your bank account swell in due time.

How to Post Memorable Content

You need to create posts that will stick in people's minds for a while. Here are some ways you can do this:

Take unique and interesting photos.

This may seem so obvious, but simply taking good pictures is one of the best ways to get followers on Instagram. Instagram is flooded with pictures of people's cats and meals, so have well-shot photos to set yourself apart. Let the pictures you take related to your audience fully. People are hesitant to follow you if you always post images they can't relate to. It doesn't have to be a "perfect" photo to be good. Good photos are more human, and any imperfections make them more so.

Put a boundary on "selfies." You can post some 'selfies' on Instagram, but don't let them dominate your account. Your followers don't want to see you but rather want to see your photos. You can seem narcissistic if you post constant selfies, and this can put off many followers. Sad as it may be, there is an exception to this if you are very attractive. Posting attractive pictures of your gorgeous self can drive many followers to your account. Still, don't let this take over your content!

Post Every Day

You need to have a new post every day and post reasonable several times if possible. Your presence must be felt all the time. With this, your follower's list will grow every day.

Add filters

Instagram became so popular because of the filter options. These filters fine-tune the colour of your photos and give them a more "real" feel. There is a variety of filters available on Instagram, so feel free to try out several until you identify the one that works well with your photo. Don't use the same filters too often, or your images will start to seem too similar. #nofilter is a popular hashtag on Instagram; if the picture is too striking to even need a filter, use it!

Place captions on every photo

You will be amazed at how fast you can turn an okay photo into a remarkable one with a good caption. Your viewers' attention is grabbed by using a caption. The more people you make smile or laugh using a caption, the more you'll retain them as followers. Cute captions or jokes are particularly trendy.

Utilize apps for extended editing control

While you can slightly edit images on Instagram, there are many apps for both Android and iOS that can provide a lot more tools. Use these apps to darken, brighten, crop, add effects, text, and so much more.

Popular editing apps are Afterlight, Photo Editor by Aviary, Bokehful and Overgram.

Create collages

A fabulous way to show a collection of images or progression is to make a collage to post on Instagram. You can do this using several apps, including InstaCollage, PicStitch and InstaPicFrame.

Post your photos at a good time

Since Instagram is an extremely popular service, your followers' feeds are probably constantly updated. Post your photos at the right time for them to be seen by as many people as possible. Make sure you post photos in the morning and after the end of normal work hours. Instagram photos normally stay around a person's feed for 4 hours so if you want your followers to actually see your images, avoid posting them in the middle of the night.

Most Beautiful Photos

Not only do you need to post consistently, but you also need to post beautiful images, which are instrumental to increasing your Instagram followers. You can even be featured in media houses for outstanding photos. You need to inspire people through your photos and not shock them out of your account.

Avoid Posting All Your Photos at Once

The necessity to post photos regularly does not mean you post all the photos you have taken at one go. If you want to post more than one photo a day, make sure they are spread out in the day. Share one photo every three to four hours. You don't want to make your followers oversaturated with images-keep them yearning for more. Don't just dump all of your photos at the risk of making your followers start passing over them.

Pick up an Insta-Style

Like most successful Instagrammers, you need to develop a signature style for your photos.

Whichever technique or filter you choose, make sure your photos stand out from the crowd.

Chapter 3: Make money through binary options

What are the options?

Options are financial securities that give the consumer the opportunity, but not the responsibility, on or before a certain date, to purchase or sell an underlying financial commodity at a certain amount. Just as you know, with specified terms and conditions, options are like every other financial asset or instrument. It is important to note that options are not assets themselves, but their values are derived from other financial assets such as stocks, hence the name derivatives.

Two styles of choices are primarily available; call and place. Call options grant you the opportunity to purchase an underlying one at a given price on or around a specific date in the future, but not the responsibility. Call investors are betting that the value of the commodity will grow in the future and thereby allow them the ability to make market profits.

On the other side, placing options gives the customer an opportunity, but not the duty, to sell an underlying commodity during a specified time at a specific amount. Placement buyers conclude that rates are expected to collapse in the immediate term.

Why options trading?

Options have been branded as some of the riskiest investment ventures. However, over the past decades, participants in the options market have tremendously grown. Why would an investment vehicle think to be so risky to gain such popularity? There are several benefits that are attributed to this, but let us shift focus on the two main reasons why people use options hedging and speculation.

1. Speculation

Speculation is better understood if thought of as betting on the price of an underlying asset. People base their beliefs on what the security price will be in the future as the market adjusts itself and make a bet on the predicted market movement. The use of options for speculation is what makes options a risky venture. You not only have to be accurate in determining the direction of the market movements but also the timing and size of such movements. Let's say you predict that the price of Microsoft stocks will likely rise in the next three months; you can buy the call option, which will enable you to buy the stocks at a lower price and sell them at a higher price. If the market moves in your favor, you can make substantial gains. However, if the market movements do not favor you, you lose 100% of your investments (options price).

2. Hedging

Options can be an insurance policy for your investments. You can use options to hedge your investments against a downturn. For example, if you assume you wish to take advantage of the upside of technology stocks like Microsoft, you can buy a put option and take advantage of the upside keeping the stocks safeguarded against any downturn.

Key point/action step

Investing is all about determining the kind of investor you are and the goals you hope to achieve in investing. When investing in options, you have two main reasons for investing; to either hedge or speculate. It is important that you determine your reason for investing in order to invest wisely.

Types of binary options

There are many types of binary options available to you as an investor. Interestingly, the most common types of binary options not only confuse new traders but also experienced ones. I will go slow just to ensure that you get this information clear.

1. Digital binary options

Under this, we have call/put and up/down options.

Call options: You place a call option if you believe that the price will rise above the entry price.

Put options: You use this if you believe that the price will not rise above the entry price.

With up/down options, you only need to predict the direction of the price movements when you entered the market. Will it move *up/down?*

2. Touch binary options

These types of binary options come with predefined rates needed to win the trade as opposed to the trading participant just predicting the direction of the price movement. Here, you predict a level of decrease or increase it will reach (touch) and the level it will not reach (no touch). Please note that these types of binary options only trade when the market is closed, mostly during weekends. If the market touches or passes the specific level by 1700GMT on Monday, you get your returns. No-touch pays when the level defined is not reached.

3. 60 seconds option

Are you the type that gets excited by quick rewards? Perhaps this is your best bet. This option expires in 60 seconds. With this, it is easy to predict price movements. Basically, I usually recommend this option for traders who wish to profit quickly from a trending market.

4. Boundary options

This is sometimes also called range options. It differs from digital options in that two-level supper, and lower are defined. The asset must stay inside this boundary for a trader to receive any payout. This method is ideal for stable markets when trading inside the boundaries and volatile markets when trading outside the defined boundaries.

Key point/action step

As you have seen in this chapter, there are different types of binary options that you can invest in; hence, it is important to choose wisely. My advice would be to start small with binary options that are easy, for instance, the boundary options that give you more leeway when it comes to anticipating price movements. However, it is up to you to choose the most suitable option to trade-in depending on the returns you are looking for. If you are the adrenaline junkie kind of investor, then the 60-second option is most suitable for you.

Chapter 4: Social media advertising

There are a great many ways to earn money through social media. What we'll discuss for this chapter are the more straightforward methods of making money from your social media accounts.

More than 50% of all internet users all over the world go online for social media. This goes without saying that websites like Facebook and Twitter are huge opportunities for advertising and marketing, and many have taken advantage of the situation by allowing people to earn by displaying advertisements on their profiles.

This is especially profitable for people who have large networks and can be considered 'influencers.' Influencers are those who have a great number of followers and therefore have more powerful recommendations.

Earning can work in several ways. Once you display a Facebook ad, you can earn when someone clicks on the link, makes a purchase and leaves their mobile number or email address.

One can also go for paid tweets such as SponsoredTweets.com. As the name suggests, you get paid when your followers click on promotional links via Twitter.

Pros: Displaying Facebook ads can give you around two cents per click, depending on your arrangement with the advertiser. Sponsored tweets can earn you $6 for one tweet for 2000 followers and can reach up to $1000 for those with a massive following. Given the amount of time that you actually spend on your social media accounts, the rate is fair enough.

A good thing about displaying ads is that you are totally in control of the content that you wish to display. This is also an opportunity to help your followers by making quality recommendations while earning at the same time.

Cons: What seems to work for social media ads can also work against it. Most people really don't like ads, and so coming up with advertising links that are catchy enough to warrant attention may be tricky. Too much hard selling can also turn off some of your followers. It may not be as effective for people who have not yet established a large network of followers.

Social media advertising can be a very lucrative venture; however, it also highly depends on the extent of your social network.

Chapter 5: Stock trading

If you find yourself with more saved cash and an appetite for risk, stock trading may be a good venture for you. To describe it simply, stock trading involves buying shares of certain companies for a particular price, then selling them afterward for a profit when the value of these companies rises.

While it does sound easy, comprehensive research must be done before one engages in stock trading as it's not uncommon for people to lose their hard-earned money when the economy stumbles, and the prices of companies suddenly crash. Smarter traders can get profits of as much as 600% in three years, but this is backed by long years of experience and the 'feel' of the stock market.

Here are a couple of tips to earn extra money from stock trading.

Be in it for the long haul. Patience has always been a virtue, and the same holds true for stock trading. You will need to learn to apply the "buy at the low and sell at the high" law, and it requires a lot of patience to keep yourself from buying just because everyone else is buying because chances are the price maybe a little too high, and it will affect your profits.

You also cannot expect a 30% profit right away in your first year of trading, as it may take five years for you to truly realize your profits.

Buy great companies. One of the things that make stock trading a hit is a fact that your earnings depend on how well your company performs. That being said, a great deal of research must be done on a company before you decide to buy a piece of it. Does it have a good management team? Does it have years of experience to show for its stability? How profitable is it? Many experienced investors say that you should only buy a company that you truly know about for you to understand how it will be affected by key events.

Diversify. Another good tip is to not keep your eggs in the same basket. Do not focus all your investment on a single company to keep yourself from crashing with it when unexpected events take place. It is always a good practice to invest in various industries to create a buffer for your investments.

Chapter 6: Blogging and freelance writing

Blogging

Blogging is one of the most common platforms for web content on the internet and can be done by almost anyone. It is a form of social networking that allows you to create your own comprehensive content where you can showcase whatever you wish.

Blogspot and WordPress are some of the leading blog posts where people can sign up for free, and it allows anyone to publish their content online. If you have a knack for writing, this one is for you. You can post a wide array of content, from blow by blow accounts of how your day went, reviews of the latest movie you watched, opinions about current events, social commentary, book reviews, advice for mothers, shared experiences about pets and many more. Writing can be done for self-expression or to share experiences that you believe can help other people.

As fun as it sounds, establishing a blog isn't a walk in the park because you will need time and commitment to update it with quality content to keep readers coming back. Junk content that is simply copied from other web pages will easily be disregarded as plagiarized content and will not help the reputation of your site. It is also recommended to find a niche topic that you can focus on so as to target a specific brand of readers and establish a regular following.

A golden rule for web content: quality is king. If your readers find that your website offers something that they cannot easily find with other webpages, they will keep coming back. More readers mean a better reputation for your blog and, therefore, higher potential earnings.

Earning through blogging can be done by leasing your webpage space to advertisers, by writing sponsored reviews or blog posts about particular companies, or by selling actual products.

When you gain a following, people keep coming back to your page. The more traffic you get, the more attractive your page becomes to advertisers because they would want to take advantage of your page views and use it for advertising their product.

Using this concept, various sites offer bloggers the ability to display advertising banners on their webpage and get paid for them. There are hundreds of sites that offer these services, and some of the most popular are Infolinks, SiteScout (formerly Adbrite), and Clicksor.

You can get paid from $0.01 to $2 per click, depending on the value of the banner. The more traffic you get, the higher chances of people clicking on the banner link, and therefore the more money you get.

Other companies pay for impressions, meaning visitors really don't need to click on the ad for you to earn; they simply have to 'see' it. This has much lower payout rates but is also more convenient to use. Bloggers strategize on the placement of their ads to come up with more clicks and more impressions.

Google AdSense is one of the leading providers of blog advertising. They are the most popular; they provide the highest payouts but are also the strictest. It is recommended that you purchase a top-level domain (www.ebook.com instead of www.ebook.blogspot.com) for them to approve your request. They also go for top-notch quality as all pages with traces of plagiarism or copied content are immediately disqualified. They also strictly screen the nature of content that they approve to ensure that it only provides quality information for potential readers. If one passes through the rigorous screening of AdSense and keeps working on improving their blog quality and traffic, they can expect earnings of $0.15 to $15 per click, with most getting up to $48 for 1000 visits, the highest among all advertisers.

For those who have established a reputation with their blog — if you are a mom known for providing valuable baby-care advice, a girl known for fabulous taste in clothing, or a guy popular among bloggers for keenly observing gadget updates — some companies may want to bank on your influence in the blogosphere by sending you free products to review or by asking you to create a write up about their brand for a fee.

This can be a tricky line to tread, however, as some readers may get 'turned-off' when they find that you are being paid by companies to make positive reviews. A good way to work around this is by providing 'full-disclosure' to your readers by telling them if a particular post was sponsored by a brand. You may also want to keep your tone from getting too patronizing to keep your blogger's integrity intact. This way, the trust system between you and your reader is maintained. Another great thing about blogging is that the manner in which you create your posts and how you build your reputation is entirely up to you. Therefore, anything that happens is really under your responsibility.

Another great way to monetize your blog is by selling products. You may have some handmade crafts that others may find useful or a friend who knows a great supplier of accessories and clothing. Instead of renting an actual physical store, you can just post your goodies on your blog, advertise them on your social networking sites and receive orders from people. Selling with this method normally involves having the products delivered to your customers, so make sure that you also know the procedure for shipment.

A lot of people have earned a living by selling online products and relying on social media and word of mouth for their advertising. It's a pretty hassle-free method because your online space is mostly free, and you invest in your product and seller reputation alone.

Blogging is a great way to earn money online, but it takes passion and commitment to keep it going because the internet is flooded by all types of bloggers, and sometimes it takes a special flair to stand out.

Blogging is not as easy as it seems, but if you've got what it takes, it can also be the most rewarding.

Freelance Writing

Freelance writing is another way to earn online through the power of the pen—or in this case, the keyboard. Several bloggers venture to freelance writing and vice versa, while a lot of them actually juggle being both. The key difference between blogging and freelance writing is that with the former, you are in full control of the layout and content, and you write for your readers on your terms. Freelance writing, on the other hand, is pretty much like outsourcing your talent for their purpose, and therefore all articles are written on the client's terms.

It may be easier or harder, depending on which side of the fence you're on. But freelance writing will definitely give you a more reliable stream of income once you've got the hang of it. Beginners can start on sites like Odesk.com or Elance.com, where potential clients and freelancers can meet to discuss terms and gain an interface for communication. The more experienced ones eventually gain contacts of their own and can get projects for higher rates.

Articles can range from a simple 400-word description of products or 30-word description of hotels to 4000-word essays or long sets of blog posts. Formatting and tone of writing can also vary, which will require flexibility and good writing skills. A strong command of grammar and spelling is a basic requirement, along with the ability to consistently meet deadlines. This also includes the patience required for hours and hours of research.

Freelance writing can be as demanding as a day job or even more. However, it still allows you to manage your own time and decide which projects to accept and which to set aside for a later time, as long as you meet the expectations of your client.

Beginners can earn about $30 to $50 an hour, while the more serious ones can earn as much as $80 for an hour and even $2000 for a month.

While these sound like really good money, one must be aware that the life of a freelance writer is anything but easy. Here are a few tips that one should bear in mind when aspiring to become a freelance writer.

Get ready for rejections. Because of the increasing level of competitiveness that this industry requires, one must be ready to experience multiple rejections of their articles. Remember that they are not rejecting you as a person, only your work. Only when you are able to resist taking rejections personally will you be able to hope to make a living out of freelance writing.

Keep your reputation clean. Your reputation as a freelancer can either make or break you. Being able to consistently submit deadlines, work according to your agreement with the client and provide quality work are sure-fire ways to boost your chances of being referred to new clients.

Socialize. Go out, meet people and socialize. This is another way to develop networks and attract potential clients. Learn to market yourself.

Set your goals. Are you content with making $1000 a month, or would you like to earn $2000 or more? Set your goals according to your family situation; if you find that you can get a lot of more than 8 hours a day for freelance writing and that you would like to earn a significantly larger amount, then you should go for higher-paying clients and better writing gigs.

Seek help. Hundreds of websites are available for freelance writers who would like to improve their craft or would like to get the hang of the technical matters involved in the trade. Take advantage of these groups in order to meet fellow writers and keep yourself motivated.

Chapter 7: E-book publishing

If you are a book lover or enthusiast, at one point in your life, you may have dreamed of publishing your own book and being a world-renowned author. You might have sniggered at the thought back then because getting published seemed too far-fetched and ambitious. What if you learned that you can now be a full-fledged author of your own book for real?

The landscape for book-reading had changed quickly since 2012 when e-books outsold hardbound covers for the first time. More and more people have been turning to e-books because of their easy accessibility and portability. In no time, self-published authors gained popularity as well. Digital publishers are making it unbelievably easy for people to publish their own books, and many are taking advantage of this opportunity. Several authors are finding themselves easily selling a thousand e-books a month and are definitely outselling their hardbound counterparts.

If you have an idea sitting in the dark corners of your mind for quite some time, now is the best time to write that e-book, and who knows, it might just give you your first million! Here's a rundown of how:

Write. There's an initial draft that is basically your brain spilled over pages of chaos, a review draft that finally organizes your thought and develops what you really want to say, and the polished editorial draft ready for publishing.

This is, of course, the most important part of the process because, without publish-worthy content, your book will not sell a dime. Focus your thoughts and define your goal straight up — would you like to entertain, inform or inspire?

Formatting. This involves making use of the digital publisher format for your e-book and coming up with a cover. The design of the cover is critical for people to take an interest in your eBook. Take note that it also must be attractive even as a thumbnail because that's how your eBook will initially be presented.

A lot of self-published authors try to design their own covers with awful results. It is recommended to hire a professional cover designer to create a more polished look for your book. If you're going to earn thousands of dollars from it, you might as well invest, right?

Publish and Promote. Head over to your digital publisher, login to your account and follow the pre-defined steps to publish your e-book. You must have your tax info ready for royalties and legality purposes.

Pricing is a very important aspect. Most e-books are priced at $2.99 to $9.99. However, it is found that most readers buy e-books in the $2.99 to $5.99 price range. Price it too high, and no one will buy it, but if you price it too low, you may not gain enough profit.

There are many digital publishers out there like Nook, iBook's, and Smashwords; however, they have already established themselves as one of the most credible sites for online transactions. The intensive feedback system is top of its class, and they help to extend the reach of your book even to people who have no idea who you are.

Promoting the book is critical to the success of your e-book because no one will buy it if they don't understand that it exists. Make extensive use of social media, offer incentives for every purchase, or advertise it in online forums and blogs. Take advantage of the digital nature of e-books to spread awareness. It may take a lot of work, but it's definitely worth it.

Publishing e-books is a great way to leave a legacy on your passion or expertise. Now is the best time to do it!

Chapter 8: Make your own video games

Your Debut into The World of Making Video Games

I am very tempted to tell you that the video game industry is a gold mine waiting for you to prospect, and indeed, it is. I am also tempted to tell you that video game creation is only a success story only for big game companies, but alas, I will not. Why? Because I would be telling you a lie. In the interconnected technology-driven world, which is where we live, anyone, and I mean anyone, can create a video game.

Do not get me wrong; I am not necessarily proclaiming video game creation success to all. I am merely stating the fact that thousands of people across the globe have been able to make their own games. Here is another fact; long gone are the days when video games had only two platforms: computers and gaming consoles. Today, with the advent of mobile technology, video gaming has gone mobile. With 98% of the world's population being owners of a mobile phone, it is only right that the video game industry would take advantage of this. Again, today, there are more mobile phone-based games than there are computers or gaming consoles in the world. What does this mean?

It means that the fruits are ready for the picking and that the pickings are in plenty. It means that if there ever were a time to get into video games production, now would be it. Contrary to popular belief and media hype, you do not need to be a geek with 'mad' coding or programming skills to create a video game (this does help, though). Anyone, even you, can create a video game. All that you require to create a game today is a bit of know-how, a lot of passion, and tons of patience. I am not promising that your video game will be an overnight sensation. I am also not promising that the journey will be easy. In fact, it may be very hard. What I promise you is that by the time we are through, you will be in a better position to create video games and well on your way to making some money from your video game creations.

Key point/action step

Although it is possible to make your own video games, you need creativity, passion, and patience if you are to become a success story.

After writing up your concept, hashing it out, and reflecting on it, it is time to fuel that enthusiasm train. Unless you are a serious video game creator with a few thousand dollars to fork out and some experience in pro programming, Unreal 4 Engine is not for you, albeit being one of the best video game creation engines. For the rest of us, who do not want to start from scratch, neither do some serious coding, we must rely on the help of software. Fortunately, the web is full of free and premium video game creation software. What I have found is that in a world of choice, most people are unsure of what to choose. It is important to point out that most of the software available each has different features, merits, and demerits. Your choice of software is entirely dependent on your game creation needs and level of expertise. I must also point out that you can do much using the available software that we will discuss shortly.

Before we move on to that, you are probably wondering why you should use an engine. Why not program the game by hand. I can give you a couple of reasons. However, I shall give you just one substantial reason. Engines provide a host of developmental tools, which aid and simplify the creation process. Furthermore, they are time efficient and less complex compared to hand programming. An engine also makes it easier to manipulate your AI (artificial intelligence), sound, and graphics.

Before I give you that list of software, I have to point out that some software is best suited for 2D graphics while others work best for 3D graphics. Above all, and regardless of your engine choice, most engines do come with tutorials to guide you in usage and creation. Here are the engines you can try to use.

Game maker: Platform-Windows and Mac OS X

The game maker engine is a product from YOYO games. It is a comprehensive engine well suited to help you create beautiful games without necessarily being a programming whiz kid. However, the program does require some getting used to (learning curve). Fortunately, the program does have a tutorial, manual, and a very vibrant user base and community ready and willing to provide you with answers to pressing questions. Unfortunately, only the light version, which does not allow for more robust features such as export, is free. For the premium version, you may have to pay up upwards of $500. Additionally, I have found the engine interface to be a bit lacking in terms of design. One of the more outstanding features of the software, both the free version and the premium version, is that you can port your game to different operating systems such as android, iOS, desktop, and HTML 5 (Web) with no basic knowledge of scripting or coding. This makes it an outstanding tool for a beginner.

Construct 2: Platform- Windows

If you liked Game Maker, then you will most definitely like Construct 2. Like Game Maker, construct 2 is also a premium engine that comes with its own user base, tutorials, manuals, and active community. Unlike Game Maker, construct 2 does not offer a free version. Instead, they offer a free 30-day trial of the full engine. Because the engine base is HTML 5, it is the best alternative to web animation tools such as Adobe Flash or Java. Using this engine, you can create beautiful 2D games that you can easily port to Windows, Linux, and Mac PCs, as well as Firefox Marketplace, Chrome Web Store, and the iOS and Android app stores. This means your games can be available on many different platforms. Unlike Game Maker, construct 2 has an appealing and robust user interface. Additionally, the engine has an in-built event system that allows you to instantly program actions and movements. The premium software costs about $120. However, if you want to use the commercial package of the engine, you will have to pay $400.

Stencyl: Platform- Linux/OS X/Windows

Stencyl is probably the most popular engine. More than 120,000 developers, with over 10,000 games published games across the globe used it. In its simple form, the engine does not require any programming skills. However, if you are tech-savvy, you can write code within the program to create more advanced features and functions. The engine has a drag-and-drop feature that adds to the easy use of the engine. Unlike all the other engines we have looked at thus far, Stencyl is not an all-out by. Instead, it works on a subscription basis; a $200 annual subscription basis; the $200 is for the most expensive (and comprehensive) package.

The engine offers cheaper discounts for students and game design experimenters. Because of the subscription nature of the engine, developers tout it as the easiest way to make some quick money (this means that the engine is commercially driven), rather than it being a fun way to experiment with video game designing. This does not mean that once you create your game, you have to submit it to them for sponsorship (which they offer)!

Flixel: Platform-Open source

Flixel is an open-source video game creation engine. This means that regardless of how you intend to use it (for commercial or personal purposes), it is completely free. This engine is very versatile. You can use it to create a wide range of 2D vector animations. The software itself runs on the backbone of ActionScript 3, an object-oriented programming language. ActionScript 3 adds a wide range of development tools to the program. These tools allow you to customize the engine. If you are looking to create filmstrip games or 'epic' 2D animation with side-scrollers, this is the 'it' engine. However, I have to point out that despite its versatility, Flixel cannot handle 3D modelling. On the other hand, I also have to point out that the tile-maps at your disposal in the engine are fulfilling and intuitive. Additionally, the engine has a plethora of camera functions; the in-built save game function and the pathfinding design all make this software one worth trying. Because the software is open–source, it has a bit of a C-style programming learning curve. I must point out that this should not stop you from using the engine. Why not? Because the open-source nature of the platform also means it has a wide user base and a thriving community.

Unity: Platform- OS X/Linux/Windows

If your aim is to make outstanding 3D video games on a budget, Unity is the choice for you. Unity is an outstanding fully-fledged design/development suite. The engine has a free version for personal use. However, for the commercial version, you must pay $1,500, i.e., if your aim is to create commercially viable games. Let not the money worry you, as the free version of the engine is something to behold too. The software, even the free version, can port to up to 10 different platforms, not limited to mobile and desktop. It is also capable of delivering crispy clear video and audio.

Key point/action step

Regardless of which engine/software you opt for, you will need to familiarize yourself with it fully if you really want to derive the most benefits. Therefore, I recommend you create your video game with a starter mentality. Additionally, if there are functions you are not sure of, turn to the online user community. They (community members) have a wealth of knowledge and are always willing to share

How to Publish and Market Your Indie Video Game

With more and more developers publishing games out to a hungry lot of gamers, generating downloads and sales for your games is harder than it has ever been. Do not despair; here are some tips to publish your game and get it noticed.

Publishing your game

Like any other store in the category of apps, your best chance for success in publishing your app is variety. Depending on the platform of your indie game, submit it to as many stores as you can find. This will ensure that more people get a chance to view or download it. Additionally, when publishing your video game, make sure that you fill out every single detail.

When you visit a store for submission, there is usually a game heading (what most of us call Meta tag), a game description, and an overview. Make sure to fill out all the fields. Also, make sure that you fill everything out correctly using keyword-rich sentences. What do I mean? If you are filling out the heading of your game, make sure it is something relevant to the scope of your game. If you are filling the description and overview field, view it as a marketing platform. It is your chance to tell users why they should download or purchase your game and what makes it different. Publishing your game is very standard and uncomplicated.

A key point you must note and a mistake that many developers make is that they fail to post their game in the right category within the store. If your game is a racing game, make sure you specify the category to increase your chances of discovery.

Marketing your game

Marketing your game is more difficult than it sounds. Moreover, it is the single most important thing to do if you are not creating video games for the fun of it. Therefore, you must create a marketing plan. A video game marketing plan is no different from any other product-marketing plan. You must set out well-defined goals and timelines by which you want to achieve those goals. You must also set out a marketing budget and resources (time, workforce etc.). If you do not have the money to hire someone to market the game for you, here are a few things you can do to enhance your total download and sales revenue.

Use social media- Social media is a vibrant marketplace that may have a great positive effect on the total sale and download of your game. If you have many friends on social media, share the game with them first and ask them to share the game with others. This is especially effective if the game is a free version. If your video game has a price tag on it, share the link to the video game with all your friends and ask them to download it. Additionally, social media also has very many developer groups. Join a few of them and contribute to topics. When you have racked up some points, tell the members that you just developed a game and you would love their support. In most cases, programmers are supportive of each other, and you will get some sales.

Use Forums- Forums are also another way to drive up your sales and downloads. They are especially effective because they provide a dedicated user base. For example, if your game is a racing one, you can join a developer's forum that caters to the racing niche.

Here, you will find many people willing to download and try your game.

Create a website- This is very critical to your marketing. Most users will often time visit the website of a game they want to buy before they download it. They do this so that they can get more information on the game. Additionally, owning a website dedicated to your game sends a message of professionalism. Additionally, a website gives you more play with keywords and search engine optimization. This can be a gold mine for download and potential sales.

Key point/action step

If you are developing a video game for fun, you can simply publish your game and wait for users to try it. However, if you are doing it for a piece of the $97 billion, you must invest some money into marketing.

Chapter 9: Web industry freelancing and art of domain flipping

With almost all stores and transactions now going online, there is a great demand for people who are able to deal with the more technical aspects to securing their online presence. Web professionals are quite like the carpenters, civil engineers and architects of the online world. And so, if you have a good command of this field and would like to earn extra online, here are a couple of things you can do:

Create tutorials. There are a lot of web enthusiasts who would love to learn how to set up a website, create a good blog design or deal with servers. One can set up a blog and provide quality and targeted tutorials and earn by blog advertising, or readers can also pay a fee for your expertise. Just make sure that people get what they pay for. Earnings can range from $50 to $150.

Design web pages and blogs. The design of a website goes beyond what it 'looks like' but also deals with the interface and ease of navigation. It takes technical knowledge to correctly configure these. You can offer these services to aspiring bloggers or start-up companies.

Selling templates, patterns and icons. If you have a great eye for design and love tinkering with patterns and graphics, you can put up some of your designs for sale. Sites like Theme forest allow you to post your original works, and interested users can buy them directly from the site. This is a great way to produce passive income from your creativity.

Keep in mind, though, that coming up with profitable designs takes years of experience to pull off as it involves an intricate play of shapes, colours and lines.

Finding bugs. In an era of increasing cybercrime, larger companies realize the value of fool-proof software that can prevent hackers from taking advantage of their efforts. Because of this, they offer a hefty amount of cash for people who find vulnerabilities in their codes.

James Forshaw was rewarded $100,000 by Microsoft in 2013 for finding a potential security flaw in one of their software. Bugcrowd is a community of similar people specializing in finding coding glitches. It's pretty much positive reinforcement for people who have incredible skills in order to put their talents to good use instead of resorting to hacking.

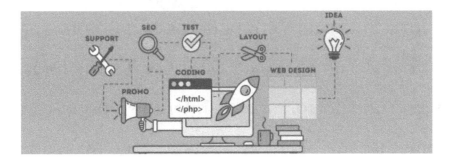

The Art of Domain Flipping

Think of 'domains' as addresses to a house. This refers to the site address of your webpage, like www.ilovethisebook.com, for example. However, to get this address for yourself, you will have to buy it from a web host and domain providers so you could own it. This prevents someone else from the opposite side of the world from putting up a page named www.ilovethisebook.com because that domain name is already yours.

So, what if you have gotten so successful and realized that you would like to rename your site to www.ilovethisebooksomuch.com? You will have to buy this domain again and leave your former webpage address to expire.

This will allow the happy lady from the opposite side of the world to finally own a website named www.ilovethisebook.com.

Domain flippers work in between these transactions to make profits. You can go through a list of the unregistered domain in sites like GoDaddy and look out for expired domain names that may be of great value for someone you know. You can purchase www.ilovethisebook.com for about $70, then send an email to a happy lady who would gladly pay you $200 for it. Bravo! The profit is made!

The key in earning through this method is being observant of current trends and insightful for things that may spark interest among people, purchasing domains while their value is still low, then selling it at a great price when you find it most profitable.

It definitely involves risk as you may encounter having to sell domains for zero profit. However, the rewards you get in the process may make this worth a try.

Chapter 10: Some other ideas

Turn Passion to Profit

" What do you really want to do?"

This is one of the most daunting life questions that hit us some time in our teenage years and stretches up until forever. Some people find the answer sooner, and others never really find out. Circumstances often lead us to do things that we'd rather not, and necessity tells us that we cannot always do what we want because the cool things don't always bring food to the table.

What if life finally granted you the opportunity to work on what you've always wanted?

The internet is a world without boundaries. It finds value in the smallest of things, reward your grandest efforts and grants you the possibility of reaching out to all corners of the earth. What may not work in your town may be a hit on a city that is miles away from you. This is a stellar opportunity to finally explore what you've always wanted, feed it to the world wide web and even earn from it! All in the comforts of your home!

Many people have followed their passion and have now gone on to become professional artists, writers, consultants and the like. Do not hesitate to explore your own.

Get Paid for Your Reviews

Do you remember spending a whole day debating with girlfriends on the phone on which makeup was better or what brand of shampoo was the best? Looks like you can actually earn from it!

Again, it all boils down to marketing and advertising. Companies would love to know what you think of their product and are willing to pay you for your opinion.

Vindale Research is an online shopping site that pays you for posting reviews about items that you have bought from their site. You can expect to get paid up to $75 both for answering reviews and surveys on their site. You can make withdrawals via PayPal to ensure the security of your information.

Other websites pay you to review other items like User Testing for website interface reviews ($10 per review), Shvoong for reviews about newspapers, academic papers, books and random articles (payout depends on revenue of the product).

Review Stream is another popular pay-for-review website that pays $2 for every review on hot topics and also gives additional points when people rate up to your review.

There are a great many legitimate sites that offer payment for each review you give their products; now, isn't that a better way to spend all that energy raving or ranting about various consumer products?

Pay-for-review is another targeted approach for earning extra money. It is a great feedback system that the common consumer can use to reach out to retail companies in order to improve the very products we use.

Getting paid for sharing what you think about your latest purchase seems to be a neat idea, yes?

The Era of Mobile Apps

The smartphone and tablet market are now saturated with apps of all shapes and sizes. While smartphone designs and capabilities are all the craze right now, mobile apps are quickly catching up because they allow you to use your phone for several functionalities that the manufacturer wasn't able to include.

There's an app that measures your heart rate, an app that reads your horoscope for the day, an app that gives directions, an app that plays dice and not to mentions the gazillions of games that are available both in Android's Playstore and I phone's Appstore. The most successful of apps are known to be earning thousands of bucks per month out of user purchases, and believe it or not, Candy Crush is actually earning $947,000 every day. Incredible!

What attracts a lot of people is that it is open to everyone with the right number of tools and knowledge. In spite of the saturated market, people still love to create something that others can use or have fun with, quite similar to publishing e-books. And there's always that hope of being the next viral thing and waking up a millionaire the next day. Remember Flappy Bird?

Creating a mobile app entails a complicated web of wireframing, data integration, user-interface development and design, server-side logic and user management, among others. But the bottom line is to create an app that can delight, entertain or be greatly useful for specific applications.

The interface of the app must be designed in an appealing and engaging manner following the modern laws of design and user-friendliness. It has to be comprehensively tested and refined with zero to minimal bugs.

Android will let your apps launch untested in the Playstore, while iPhone requires all apps to undergo a review process that takes about a week. Once it's out there, your apps will be tested through user reviews and purchases.

One thing that developers forget, though, is to advertise their apps. This is essential if you really want to earn.

Bookkeeping

Another technical skill that could be put to use is bookkeeping. This basically entails keeping a clean record of all the cash flow details of a particular company or individual. This includes keeping track of all invoices, receipts, earnings and payables. This is gaining increasing momentum in several countries because more and more entrepreneurs are trying to enter businesses without knowing how to streamline their cash flow. This is critical to businesses because it allows you to keep track of your collectibles and your deadlines. Unmanaged finances will only cost a business more money and a bad reputation in the future.

This type of industry is good for people who don't get bored with numbers, have an eye for detail and the integrity to keep records clean. Various online courses are now being offered for people who would like to get the hang of the industry, but one may require a couple of years of actual training before gaining enough reputation to work as an independent bookkeeper.

Armed with sufficient storage, reliable accounting software, and a great ability to organize, bookkeeping can be a great work-at-home job for people. The average bookkeeper earns $25 to $40 per hour but can also increase depending on workload and location.

Adding tax preparation services can also increase your value as a bookkeeper, and so does an accounting background. Having business cards and referrals from former satisfied clients will also boost your reputation.

Pay-to-Click Sites (PTC)

Clixsense, Probux, Neobux and Fusebux are some of the most trusted online sites when it comes to pay-to-click industries. This is by far the easiest way to earn money on the internet. It basically starts with you clicking the "Register now" button and signing up for their services; then, you start to familiarize yourself with the website interface while earning. It will not require you to pay upon registration though some of them may require an optional 'investment' for you to grow your earnings faster, although you'll do just fine even without availing of this option.

The main mechanism of earning is by clicking and watching 30-second ads and quickly moving on to the next, depending on how much you intend to earn.

Pros: This is the easiest way to earn on the internet; no experience or necessary skill sets are required, and you decide how much time you are willing to allot. They also design the site and advertisements well enough to keep you engaged and entertained during the whole session.

The product also has a community forum where users can share ideas and help in navigating the site, which makes it all the more legitimate because you are confident that other people are really using and getting paid with it.

These companies also make use of PayPal, Payza, Perfect Money, SolidTrust Pay, and Ego Pay, which allow users to receive their payment without really revealing too much financial information.

Cons: In as much as they provide the easiest ways to earn money, they also have the lowest rates of payment. Clixsense has one of the highest payouts, which is $0.02 per click.

These sites also have a minimum payout threshold, meaning you have to accumulate a certain amount before you are able to withdraw to your account. Clixsense has a minimum payout level of $10, which means you'll have to click through the ads 500 times before you are able to withdraw. That's about four and a half hours of viewing ads! As you see, it may take a long while before you are really able to withdraw a substantial amount.

Other sites offer a smaller payout threshold like Neobux that only requires $2, and Probux, for only $5. However, the rate per click is also lower.

Earning PTC ads is a great idea only when you intend for this to be an additional activity while browsing the internet. You'll also need to be extra patient with it because it will take a while before you are able to really earn.

Value in the Smallest Efforts

Companies spend a great bulk of their budget on advertising and will go to great lengths just to extend their brand reach and to understand how their consumers perceive their products. This concept has driven an online industry that allows people to earn dollars by doing very simple tasks like clicking links, answering surveys, viewing advertisements and the like. Many people are flocking to this kind of industry because of the promise of earning with very little effort.

As attractive as it is, this type of industry is also one of the most prone to abuse and scams and must therefore be examined carefully before getting involved. If you feel like the pay is way too large for the equivalent effort required, follow your gut feel and check if it is a scam.

Nevertheless, there are legitimate companies who really use these methods as part of their advertising, and it's a great deal for people who want to earn extra bucks for a couple of minutes. If you can spend a whole hour watching cat videos, then the idea of answering a 15-minute survey for five dollars shouldn't be a bad idea, yes?

No effort is too small for the internet. Everything has value.

Conclusion:

To conclude, business valuation, if done correctly, can work in your favor. That is also true for the intended buyer. Business valuation can be done in-house or through the help of certified public accountants and business valuators.

It is also very important to discuss matters about selling your business with people around you (business partners, workmates and family members) to help you cement the idea. Once a business changes hands, it is permanent until the current owner decides to sell again.

Placing value on your business and eventually selling it off is the culmination of all the years, tears and hard work of building the business and running its day-to-day operations. Some business owners are anxious about separating themselves from their own businesses. In the end, through proper business valuation, you will be able to see your business as it is. It is just an income-generating machine that you built and developed.

Remember that although this book provides you with the basic knowledge on how to place a value on your business' worth, the need for professional business valuators and certified public accountants are still necessary. The practical knowledge that they possess concerning this aspect of the business is one gained through constantly perfecting their craft.

This book aims to open your eyes to what goes behind the scenes during these transactions and help you understand the business valuation process. The simple action steps provided in each chapter and subchapters are there for you to perform on your own business.

Finally, it is imperative that you are keen on the details of your own business and are meticulous about keeping records. These records will help you find the true value of your business.

Bookkeeping and QuickBooks Made Easy

A Comprehensive Guide of 87 Useful Tricks to Hack QuickBooks and Organize Bookkeeping as a Silicon Valley Company

By

Lee Green

Table of Contents

Introduction

This book is your basic guide to bookkeeping and QuickBooks. If you are a bookkeeper and want to upgrade your skillset and learn more about the QuickBooks software, this book is just for you. You will find a comprehensive detail of all the considerations, the advantages, and the ways you can become a QuickBooks bookkeeper. If you are a beginner and managing finances interests you, you can equally benefit from this book.

In the following chapters, you will find a detailed explanation of bookkeeping and why proper bookkeeping is necessary to keep businesses afloat. With people starting their businesses by the minute, the need for accurate bookkeeping is ever in demand. Small business owners invest in good financial handling software and outsourcing their account management to bookkeepers as affording an accountant is sometimes not possible for a small business owner.

You might question that bookkeeping is not as lucrative but do not pay head to that. Yes, conventional bookkeeping is becoming outdated, but still, there is demand. Most small business owners in the US use the software QuickBooks for their financial recording. Though some business owners know how to use it and keep updated, most of them will require help with crunching numbers and outsource professional bookkeepers to do the job.

QuickBooks was launched in the year 2003 by the company Intuit. After its launch, the company has launched various versions of the software to cater to different business owners' requirements. QuickBooks usage dominates the small business market by 80%. The company provides desktop-based and cloud-based versions of the software. From 2014 onwards there is a shift in trend. Before 2014, the business owners preferred the desktop model, but after the year 2014, more and more business owners are shifting to the cloud-based versions.

A whole chapter is dedicated to explaining the QuickBooks software. We discuss in detail the entire software. The services it provides and how a small business owner can benefit from it. There is a step-by-step guide to set up and install QuickBooks into your computer or other devices. After installation, guidelines are given to setup your account and add the vendor and customer accounts. A detailed explanation about how to enter employee details and how some versions can also manage automated payroll tasks. Reading about all this will make you understand the software's entire system and objective and realize how easy it is to operate. Technology has made even the most difficult and complicated tasks simpler for us. Now, it is our job to use technology for our benefit.

After you have understood the basic functioning of the software, you might want to invest in one. But this is not as easy as just purchasing one online. There are different packages of software available for different individuals. There are four basic packages available:

- QuickBooks Online

- QuickBooks Self-Employed

- QuickBooks Desktop

- QuickBooks App

Choosing the correct package that suits your requirements is also an important and difficult decision. In this book, we give you an overview of all the available packages and their specific features. All this information will hopefully make your decision easy.

In the US, the small to mid-size business market is denominated by QuickBooks users, and the owners are always on the lookout for professional QuickBooks bookkeepers for the job. You do not have to do it full time; you can manage all the accounts as a side hustle because QuickBooks software makes everything easy. You have to setup your accounting needs in the software, and most of the work is done by the software. However, it is n0t as easy as it sounds. The software is user-friendly, but you still require basic accounting knowledge and correct usage of the program. You might consider becoming a certified QuickBooks bookkeeper.

In this book, we have also discussed how in 2021, QuickBooks bookkeepers who work online make good money. There is a whole chapter in which we discuss working part-time as a QuickBooks bookkeeper is becoming a high-paying job. The average income of a QuickBooks professional in the US is discussed along with the US's best cities where you can practice QuickBooks bookkeeping. The considerations you should keep in mind while moving base to become a bookkeeper. California is the best place to be because the money QuickBooks bookkeepers are making there is approximately $10000 more than the US average per year.

There is an entire chapter dedicated to the ways you can become a certified QuickBooks bookkeeper. Sometimes a person knows what he/she wants but is unable to do anything because of the lack of guidance. This book gives you just that, proper step-by-step guidance on how to qualify yourself to become a QuickBooks bookkeeper. It does take time and effort, but you have numerous possibilities and options once you are qualified. To become a bookkeeper, you will need a certification. There are commonly three types of certifications you can choose from:

- QuickBooks Online Certification: Basic

- QuickBooks Desktop Certification: Basic

- QuickBooks Desktop Certification: Advance

The certifications are not just a one-time feat. You must keep your certifications up to date. You will require recertification each year by taking the certification exam. These tests are expensive but worth it.

Finally, we discuss the tricks and hacks you can use to use QuickBooks efficiently and effectively. These trips and hacks make your work easier and quicker. You will have to put in fewer hours. It is always wise to use trips and hacks and make the most benefit of the latest technologies. Sometimes doing online courses and certifications enable you to learn these tricks and hacks. Therefore, it is always recommended to keep your knowledge latest and keep improving your skills. The process of learning never stops. You keep learning throughout life. In present times learning has become a necessity rather than a luxury. In the ever-changing world, you will be left behind if you do not keep your skillset updated.

We hope you are going to find this book informative and helpful for your future professional endeavors. If bookkeeping is your calling, you should pursue it. It is one of the most in-demand services in the small business and mid-size business sector.

Chapter 1. Bookkeeping

In this chapter, we will focus on the basics. We will discuss the concept of bookkeeping and how it is the one-stop solution to all your accounting needs. Before anything else, we will try to understand what bookkeeping is and its importance.

Bookkeeping is an essential part of financial management. Small business owners sometimes try to manage the bookkeeping themselves, which becomes a reason for their businesses to fail. People do not realize that bookkeeping is a full-time job. You cannot manage a business and run numbers simultaneously. For this purpose, it is always wise to hire professionals for your accounting and bookkeeping.

What is Bookkeeping?

You must have heard about the term accounting. Bookkeeping is just that; it is related to managing the accounts. This term is used for business. The management of the complete finances of a business is termed bookkeeping.

To be more specific, we say that bookkeeping involves recording all the financing situations of a business. Bookkeeping is about keeping a record of all financial transactions daily, the influx and efflux of cash, the Payroll, profits, loss, investments, return on investments, and all the decisions related to the business's finance aspect. Bookkeeping helps the business owners keep track of all the information regarding the financial transactions.

After learning about what bookkeeping is, one wonders how a business owner can do all that by themselves? Not all business owners are literate about managing their finances. So, how can a business owner manage their accounts and finances? The simple answer to this question is a bookkeeper.

Who is A bookkeeper?

Bookkeepers are professionals who are responsible for managing all the finances of a company. They keep the owners aware of their present financial situation, record all related financial data and the total transactions made.

Correct bookkeeping is important for the business owners as well as prospected investors as well. Bookkeeping information is beneficial for the government and financial institutions as well. It will give a clear overview of the economic impacts of that certain business. Big companies and individual investors tend to research before they invest their money somewhere. The best and most reliable source of this information can be found in the company books. Looking at the books, the investor will decide whether he/she wants to invest in a certain company or project. In this way, bookkeeping is important for the owners because it is like his business introduction to the investment world. The better and more accurate the bookkeeping, the more chances of investment.

(A typical Bookkeeper)

Importance of Bookkeeping

When people start a new business, they tend to neglect the importance of good bookkeeping. Finance must be taken charge from day one and cannot be neglected for a single day. Now, what does bookkeeping do? It gives the company a tangible indicator of its performance and current situation. With this information's help, it becomes easier for the owner to make proper decisions financially, revenue generated, the profits, the loss, the income goals, etc. Each transaction must be recorded; the cash influx, efflux, credits, assets, liabilities all need to be recorded.

Bookkeeping is essential to keep the business afloat. Bigger companies usually hire accountants for the financial department, but it is not always possible for small business owners. So, small business owners mostly rely on hiring a bookkeeper. There whole accounting companies from where you can outsource a bookkeeper. It is cheaper than employing a full-time accountant, and a bookkeeper can easily manage a small business account. Anyone who starts a new business should never ignore the importance of keeping a record of every dime they spent and earn. Everything should be recorded.

Type of Accounting Method

Each business model follows one of the two accounting methods.

- Cash Basis of Accounting

- Accrual Basis of Accounting

To implement the bookkeeping function properly, the business owner should decide which accounting method they will follow. There are two basic models for accounting which are mentioned above. Now, what is the difference between these two? We will try to explain:

Cash Basis of Accounting:

In this type of accounting, a transaction is only recorded when a payment or cash is received or spent.

For example, if you buy fifty units of a product and the payment will be done after two weeks. No transaction will be recorded. It will only be recorded after two weeks when the payment is made.This type of accounting model is now considered outdated in present times.

Accrual Basis of Accounting:

In accrual accounting, the expenses and revenue are put down when the transaction is made rather than when the payment is made.

We use the same example of buying 50 units of a product and payment must be made after two weeks. The record will be entered as soon as the receipt is received and will be recorded as payables. This is the more modern model for accounting and is widely accepted.

What do the bookkeepers do?

Now that you have a basic idea of who a bookkeeper is let us move to the set of responsibilities and jobs the Bookkeeper carries out. Listed are the tasks carried out by bookkeepers that make it convenient for the business owner to systematically run the business and provide a clear picture of its financial position. The responsibilities of bookkeepers include:

- Recording transactions every day.

- Sending invoices to clients.

- Keep track of payments.

- Prepare and maintain the payable ledger.

- Manage the cash flow.

- Compile and maintain all accounts.

Record the Transactions Each Day

One of the jobs of the Bookkeeper is to enter the transactions each day. These include bank transactions. Nowadays, most companies use software to manage accounts. Some software has a function to generate automated bank feeds, which makes the task easier. You must keep a check on the cash, and precious data entry time is saved.

Sending Invoices to Clients

Another responsibility of the Bookkeeper is to make receipts and invoices on purchases and send them to the clients.

Keep Track of Payments

Once the invoice is sent out, keeping a record of the payments received is also the Bookkeeper's responsibility. To keep a follow-up to receive pending payments is also the responsibility of the Bookkeeper. This is also known as being responsible for the receivable ledger.

Being Responsible for the Payable Ledger

Up to a certain amount determined by the business owner, the Bookkeeper makes the payments made on the owner's behalf. The Bookkeeper keeps records of all the payments made by the business. These include the payments to the suppliers, the extra cash available, and the other business expenses. The Bookkeeper records all this information and checks it every day.

Responsible for Managing the Cash Flow

One of the most important business rules is that a certain amount of cash is always available. The responsibility of the Bookkeeper is to always maintain the balance. This can be done by keeping a record of the day-to-day expenses and revenues. There should always be cash available for the day-to-day expenses. If the Bookkeeper suspects that the balance might be disrupted, he/she can offer advice to the owner by telling them ways to control the outflow and increase the inflow. These devices are almost always short-term fixes.

Compile All Accounts

The most important job of the Bookkeeper is to maintain the account books. The account records should all be up to date. These include all the ledgers. This is necessary for further investments and business decisions. The owner or prospect investor looks at these accounts and makes decisions according to the financial situations mentioned in the books.

How can a Bookkeeper be Beneficial for Business?

When you have a smaller business setup, it makes sense to manage your account yourself. But when the business expands, it is always a good idea to hire someone to take care of the bookkeeping. In this way, you can concentrate on expanding the business, and your Bookkeeper can take care of your day-to-day expenses. Many people do not hire a bookkeeper to save money but lose a lot of precious time in managing their account that they could be using to innovate and expand their business. Bookkeeping is a time-consuming job, and it should be left to the ones who are professionally trained to do so. They might as well do the job better and take less time. Following are listed a few benefits of hiring a bookkeeper:

Let you Focus on Your Business Strategy

As explained earlier, bookkeeping is a time-consuming task and demands attention to detail. Hiring a bookkeeper will save you all that time, and you will have plenty of time to focus on your business.

The Accounting Cost can be Saved.

If you have a small business, it is a better idea to hire a bookkeeper. If you hire an accountant, it will cost you more money and will become a liability. All the recording and accounts can be easily managed by a bookkeeper as well, and it will cost you a lot less money.

Double Check Your Cashflow

As a business owner, it is wise to always keep your eyes on the cashflow. But sometimes, you can get caught up, and in that situation, your Bookkeeper is there to tell you when you need to manage your cash flow. The Bookkeeper can warn your earlier, and you will still have time to manage the situation.

Be Informed of Current Financial Situation:

As the Bookkeeper is working on a day-to-day basis, he/she will be aware of all the business's financial situations. If you require any help and advice in this department, you can advise your Bookkeeper to have the complete information and explain the clear picture to you.

The Financial Data is Organized

In case you get hold of good software like QuickBooks, the Bookkeeper will work on the same software. The data is kept organized and transparent using the software because the margin for mistakes is highly reduced. The accountant can analyze the same data if you wish to get advice regarding business expansion and investment.

All in all, bookkeeping is particularly useful for business owners and investors alike. If you are not a businessperson and are interested in managing accounts for other small businesses, bookkeeping could be a good profession for you. The possibilities are limitless.

Chapter 2. QuickBooks Explained

With a basic knowledge of bookkeeping and what it means for small businesses, we can now discuss bookkeeping solutions. 2021 is all about solutions. Bookkeeping is a difficult task. It can be made easy with the help of accounting software. In this chapter, we are going to discuss software known as QuickBooks.

2.1. What is QuickBooks?

If you are a small business owner and you aim to reach the next level, you might want to start keeping track of your finances. Most people control their finances when they start with a business, but it becomes difficult once the business gains pace. If you wish to expand your business, you will have to become more proactive, take hold of your finances, plan your next financial moves, keep an eye on day-to-day transactions, and organize a cash inflow and outflow system. You should set up a payroll. All the administrative work should be organized. Reading all this must have given you a headache. You were thinking about making some money; how are you going to manage all the financial stuff?

It would be best if you were thankful for your stars that you live in the 21st Century and there is software available for everything. In this chapter, we are discussing accounting software that works like magic. The software is known as QuickBooks. QuickBooks is the perfect tool for your financial necessities.

2.1.1. QuickBooks

It is accounting software that has features to organize the financial aspects of small businesses. The functions of QuickBooks include:

- Recording everyday transactions

- Track and record revenue and expense.

- Report generation for planning

- Prepare bills.

- Preparation of Payroll

The software is targeted towards small to medium-sized business setups. The QuickBooks software has features that make it possible for you to manage report generation, sales, cash flow, billing, revenue, taxes, reporting and expenses. The best part about the software is that there are inbuilt templates for reports that you can easily set and customize according to your specifications. It is easy to fill in data to an already prepared template compared to create by yourself. You can take control of your finances. It is a user-friendly software, but it has a learning curve, and you must have some basic accounting knowledge to operate and use this software. To use the software effectively, you must learn and have an in-depth knowledge of the software's essential functions.

2.1.2. The History of QuickBooks

In 1983, two inventors Scott Cook, and Tom Proulx, created the company Intuit. QuickBooks is a product of this company and was first launched in 2003 and targeted to small businesses. Over the years, better and more functional versions of the software have been launched. It remains one of the most widely used financial software for small businesses in the US. Different versions of the software are available in the international markets as well.

2.2. QuickBooks Features

QuickBooks is amazing software with multiple features and functions. Here is a list of a few features of the software.

2.2.1. user Friendly

This software is super user-friendly. It is easy to use and navigate. All the financial features needed for a small to medium business are present in this one program. You do not have to record your data in different locations. This single software manages all your data.

2.2.2. Data Migration

This is a wonderful feature. If you want to transfer any data from QuickBooks to the spreadsheet, the transition is smooth. When there is a requirement to present the data on a spreadsheet, you can easily transfer all the software from the software without manually copying it.

2.2.3 Smooth Navigation

To use this software is easy because the navigation is simple. Everything is displayed clearly, and working is smooth. The program interface is clear and simple. However, you will have to learn and get used to the software before you can use it. You need to learn and understand all the financial terms and data entry methods to using this software effectively.

2.2.4. Smooth Transactions

The bank transactions are systematically recorded. Each entry you make is recorded. You can even set up regular transactions like salary payments, commissions, and bills repeated each month or every two weeks. These transactions will be automatically recorded.

2.2.5. Invoices

You can set up the invoices to be generated. The software can even generate invoices from your smartphone or tablet if they are installed with the software. You are not dependent on the computer system or laptop to generate business invoices. This feature is truly per the present requirement where everything can be achieved with a click of a button anytime, anywhere.

2.2.6. Calculate Tax

The feature of tax calculation is included in the software. To do taxes is always a tricky business. With the QuickBooks software, you can easily calculate the taxes quickly, efficiently, and accurately.

2.2.7. Projections

There is an automated feature in the software that will present you with projections. The software can generate all kinds of projections, including profits, expenses, sales etc. Getting the projections makes it easy to make financial decisions.

2.3. Set-up QuickBooks

To use QuickBooks, you must have basic accounting knowledge and your own business. To use this software, you must be organized and willing to manage your finances seriously and as a daily feature. Some people install QuickBooks, put in the money, and forget it for months. Some purchase it and never even learn how to use it. QuickBooks does not work in that manner. You must be willing to learn and be consistent. Consistency is the key.

Let us discuss step-by-step guidelines for using QuickBooks.

2.3.1. Start

The first step will be to install the software properly. For installation, you must decide how you are going to use it. When you start the program, you will have two options:

- Network

- Custom Options

You will choose the Custom settings if you use the software on only one computer and use the same computer for installations.

In case more than one computer will use the software, chose the Network setting.

After that, choose the location or folder in your PC where you wish the software to be installed. Add your details, and then set up your company file. After that, click on the QuickBooks icon on the desktop.

2.3.2. setup

As soon as you click on the QuickBooks program, you will see an Easy Setup Wizard to help you set up your company file. By following the simple instructions, you can set up your company file. If you are new to this kind of software, you will be favorable to take help from the wizard. It will make the setup smooth and easy.

2.3.3. Vendor Setup

The next step will be setting up the accounts for your vendors. You will click the Vendor Center in the toolbar placed at the top. Next, select the New Vendor option, and create a vendor account. To add a new transaction, click the New Transaction and fill in the details. You can even bring in details from MS Excel and MS Word.

Add all the vendors similarly if you have more than one.

2.3.4. Setup Employee Accounts

To set up the employee accounts, click the Employee Center. Then click the New Employee button and then add the related information. After the information, you click the button for New Transaction. Add the salary details and any other transaction related to that specific employee. For salary, you must add the date and time for each month. For that, you will click Enter Time and then add the specific time and frequency of salary. Some employers pay per month, and some pay by the week. Put in the information accordingly.

2.3.5. Set Up Customer Account

Like the vendor and employee accounts, add the customer accounts. First, you go to the customer center, then Add Customer and Job. Here you can add it as an income source. Now add the related transaction by clicking New Transaction. Here you will add the information for payments and generation of invoices. There is a link for Excel as well as Word. You can bring the information from Excel and use Word to prepare letters for the customer.

2.3.6. Setup Report Generation

Next, you will go to the Report Center. All the information added by you can be viewed here. You can also customize the kind of report you want to generate. Reports for-profits, payments and expenses can be generated separately.

Add all the employees the same way if you have more than one.

2.4. Using QuickBooks

After the set up let us try to understand the day-to-day working of the QuickBooks software. What should we expect from the software? How can we manage our finances? What is the essential feature of the software? All these questions will be answered in the following part of this book. Together we will try to understand how the QuickBooks software works.

2.4.1. Chart of Accounts

So, what can you find on the chart of accounts? It will display the company's income, liability, expense accounts, assets, and equity to assign day-to-day transactions. This is what you will find:

- All the financial information about the company. It has the balance sheets, dividend, savings, receivables, and expenses. All this can be seen in the Chart of Accounts as a list.

- All the accounts related to the business, along with the account balances and account numbers. The details of the account holder will also be shared, like the full names and contact numbers. All these accounts will appear when you click the List Menu in the QuickBooks chart of accounts.

2.4.2. Other Lists

These include the list of vendors you deal with. All your regular customers and customer accounts are listed. All the items you deal with and their inventory is listed.

How this is favorable for the QuickBooks user:

- You can manage everything in one place. You do not have to manage multiple lists and settings. All information is compiled in one place. Either it is the product inventory or the vendor; all can be managed in one place.

- When you have all the information in a single space, you can move back and forth with all the lists, account details and information. You can simultaneously manage all your financial situations together. Everything is easy to navigate and extremely user-friendly.

- Another feature is the easy addition ad deletion of details. It is simple to add new accounts, and it is equally simple to delete accounts. Anytime you want to change the existing settings, it is easily done.

- Apart from adding ad deleting details, you can also edit details. Correction and updating details are easy in this software.

2.4.3. The Reports

Report templates are already included in the software so that you can customize them according to your needs. Add the details of your vendors, customers, and items. You must add dates and times as well.

Once you start adding details accordingly and you update daily transactions and activities. The reports will be forming themselves. Anytime you feel like having an overview of your business, you can pull out reports with just one click, and the reports will be generated. These reports will help you make important financial and investment decisions.

2.4.4. payroll

QuickBooks makes it easy to manage payrolls. With the software, you add the information, and the program will itself arrange the payroll process. The software can itself manage the accounts of the employees who have tax exemption. You can customize the settings for other incentives and deductions. If you turn on the setting, the software automatically sends emails, deposits, and receipts.

More than one person can manage the payrolls in this software, the one who has purchased the software has to allow the other users on the network by assigning permission.

2.5. QuickBooks Versions

QuickBooks is available in different types and versions. Each has a different package and fee. The versions are discussed in detail in the following chapters. Here we will list down the various versions of QuickBooks software:

- QuickBooks Online

- QuickBooks Self Employed

- QuickBooks App

- QuickBooks Desktop Products

  - QuickBooks Pro

  - QuickBooks for Mac

  - QuickBooks Enterprise

  - QuickBooks Premier

Chapter 3. Choosing the Best Version of QuickBooks

With the knowledge you have gained in the previous chapters, you know that QuickBooks is a financial solutions software. It was launched 25 years ago, and it has been the top choice for financial management since 2003. If you look at the company profits, they will show you an upward trend for the last 11 years straight. In addition to that, QuickBooks is used by 80% of small business owners in the US. This information enough should convince you to invest in the software.

Once you have decided to purchase the QuickBooks software, you are faced with yet another dilemma. Which version is for you? As discussed in the previous chapter, various versions of QuickBooks are available.

The QuickBooks family has a product for everyone. Here is a quick assessment of what you may want to purchase.

- If you are self-employed, run your company alone, and are looking to invest in a cloud-based accounting system, you should invest in QuickBooks for Self-Employed.

- If you own a small business and are interested in a cloud-based accounting system, you should invest in QuickBooks Online.

- If you are a small to medium-sized business owner, you must invest in QuickBooks Desktop.

- If you are already using QuickBooks and wish to update to another version, invest in QuickBooks Apps.

One of the deciding factors in any investment is the price range and affordability. This is the approximate price of the QuickBooks Packages available, making it easy for you to decide which product is best for you and is easy on the pocket.

Version	Usage	Price
QuickBooks Online	For businesspersons who want flexible financial access. This is suitable for small to mid-size business owners.	$25 up to $150/month
QuickBooks for Desktop	Suitable for small to medium size business owners in any sector	$399.99 with a one-time payment to $1,213 for one year
QuickBooks for Self- Employed	This is suitable for individual property agents, independent vendors, and Uber	$15/ month

	workers.	
QuickBooks Mac	This is for small to mid-size businesspersons who have their business setup on MAC	$399.99 paid once

(Prices of Different Versions of QuickBooks)

3.1. QuickBooks for Self-Employed

QuickBooks Self Employed is the newest addition to the QuickBooks software versions. This is cloud-based software for financial services. It is specially designed for self-employed business owners and freelance service providers. It is ideal for independent workers like Lyft and Uber drivers. Property agents can also use it.

As this is a cloud-based program, you can access it with any computer or device with the given login.

(QuickBooks Self Employed Interface)

(Display of Reports on QuickBooks Self Employed)

Using this program, you can send data to TurboTax and track personal and business expenses from a single bank account. It also calculates the Quarterly Tax and reminds you of payment.

You will find three types of packages available for QuickBooks for Self-Employed:

3.1.1. QuickBooks Self Employed Package

Investing in this package gives you the following features:

- Users can easily connect to their bank account through QuickBooks Self -Employed

- The users can also connect to their credit cards.

- Users can track the expenses and income from the same account but can be separated into personal and business groups.

- The software calculates taxes quarterly.

3.1.2. QuickBooks for Self-Employed Tax Bundle

This offers all the services provided by the simple package with an addition:

- Users can connect to Intuit Turbo Box that enables them to pay taxes online each quarter.

3.1.3. QuickBooks for Self-Employed Live Tax Bundle

Provides all the services as the packages mentioned above with an addition that:

- Users can consult a CPA all year round.

- The users can get the services of a CPA to review taxes.

3.1.4. Benefit

It can track traveling and Mileage. You can enter trips with dates, reasons, and distance traveled. The system will automatically calculate deductions.

3.1.5. Drawback

Does not provide a service to generate invoices and online payments.

3.2. QuickBooks Online

QuickBooks Online is also a cloud-based financial solutions software. This had become exceedingly popular after 2014 when it was observed that more business owners preferred the online version over the desktop version. After that, the number of subscribers to the QuickBooks online version has been more than 1 million subscribers. This also tells us about the shift of business owners to a cloud-based system and shows their confidence in solely cloud-based software.

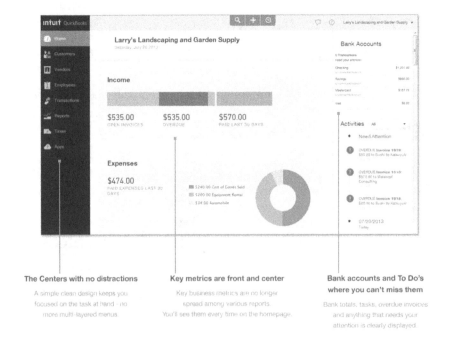

(QuickBooks Online Interface)

3.2.1. Common Features

The common features of QuickBooks Online are:

- Payable and Receivable Accounts:

The program can successfully manage expenses as well as income.

- Invoices and Bills:

It offers recurring or single-time invoices and can pay bills online.

- Management of Expenses:

The software can track all the business-related expenses.

- Reporting:

There are templates of prebuilt reports provided in the software, including the sales and tax reports. Simple Start gives 20 templates, Essentials gives 40 such templates, and gives 60 templates.

The QuickBooks online package does not need to be installed and comes in four packages:

3.2.2. QuickBooks Online Simple Start

The features provided in this package are:

- There is a single-user license.

- You can import your data from the QuickBooks Desktop version or MS Excel.

- You are entitled to consult two accounting professionals (bookkeepers and accountants)

3.2.3. QuickBooks Online Essentials

This version has all the abilities of the above version and, in addition to those capabilities, also has the following capabilities:

- The user is entitled to have 3 user licenses.

- The owner can set up user permissions to determine who is entitled to use the software.

3.2.4. QuickBooks Online Plus

All the capabilities of the Essentials version plus the following added qualities:

- Can setup 5 user licenses.

- The ability to track inventory.

- Users can create and send orders of purchase.

3.2.5. QuickBooks Online Advanced

This includes all the capabilities of the Plus version andthe following capabilities:

- Can set up 25 user licenses.

- The ability for automated bill payment.

- The user can setup customized permissions.

3.2.6. Benefits

It is available for iOS, Windows, and Android devices. It can be connected to PayPal and Shopify for transactions.

3.2.7. Drawbacks

All the functions available in the QuickBooks Desktop are not available on QuickBooks Online. This version does not allow the addition of more than one company.

3.3. QuickBooks Desktop

The QuickBooks Desktop is the most elaborated software version among all three of the versions. Most business owners prefer cloud-based financial services, but if you prefer desktop-oriented software, the QuickBooks Desktop version is for you. This version further has six more variations suitable for different types of small businesses. The six types are briefly explained as follows:

3.3.1. QuickBooks Desktop Pro:

This is good for most small businesses that are not involved in product manufacture.

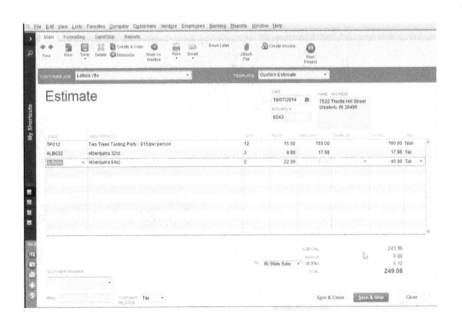

(QuickBooks Desktop Pro)

3.3.2. QuickBooks Desktop Premier:

This version is ideal for businesses involved in manufacturing, retail, and related to charity and non-profit organizations.

(Homepage of QuickBooks Desktop Premier)

3.3.3. QuickBooks Desktop Enterprise:

This is for large companies and enterprises. This version has industry reporting and a custom chart of accounts.

(QuickBooks Desktop Enterprise sales management)

3.3.4. QuickBooks Desktop Plus and QuickBooks Desktop Pro

The QuickBooks Desktop Plus and QuickBooks Desktop pro versions are sold as a yearly subscription rather than a one-time purchase. With these versions, your QuickBooks version is updated yearly, you are entitled to customer support, and your company data will be backed up.

3.3.5. QuickBooks for Mac

This is the only version compatible with Mac. It is like the QuickBooks Desktop Pro version. This is useful for most of the small businesses which are not involved in manufacturing.

3.4. QuickBooks Apps

QuickBooks Apps are applications that can be used in combination with the QuickBooks software to enhance their features. These are also known as add-on applications. These add-ons can be purchased from the QuickBooks website. Some of the QuickBooks Apps are as follows:

3.4.1. QuickBooks Payments

This can be used as an add-on for the QuickBooks desktop to add some payment functions. This app enables the business to accept payments online as well as through credit cards. This also enables emailing of invoices.

3.4.2. QuickBooks Point of Sale

This is a cloud-based application. It enables the businesses to accept credit cards, track inventory and ring up sales through a point-of-sale dashboard.

3.4.3. QuickBooks Payroll

This app enables businesses to provide salaries to up to 50 employees by cash deposit or check. Two types of versions are available:

- Self-Service Solutions

- Full-Service Solutions

The app can calculate the state, federal, and local taxes automatically.

3.5. Find the Best Version for You

QuickBooks has been a prominent player in the American market as a financial solution provider. The possibilities are numerous with this software. If you are a new business owner or plan to expand your business, QuickBooks will have a suitable version for you. But how to choose one which best suits your requirements? Here is a list of actions you can take before purchasing QuickBooks software. These activities will clear your dilemma, and the choice can be made easily:

3.5.1. Read Reviews

The best way to get a clear idea about a product is by reading reviews of people who have already used it. See which product is continually rated better. Read about the kind of services the software provides. Sometimes you get more knowledge about a product or service from reading someone's review. Always go through people's reviews and consider the products that most people are buying. Their performance must be the reason for their higher sales.

3.5.2. Take an Online Survey

When you are doing your research online, you may come across some online surveys which ask a few basic questions about your business and earnings. When you have entered your answers, the automated program will suggest the best software for you.

3.5.3. Talk to an Expert.

If you are still confused about which software to buy, try talking to an expert. A professional will be in a better position will suggest you according to your needs.

Chapter 4. The Best Way to Make Money In 2021

The year is all about small businesses and freelance work. In uncertain times everyone is pushing for a side hustle. We often have a misconception that the difficult part is setting up a business; other things follow once that part is covered. We cannot be more wrong in that approach. Though getting an idea, arranging for the finances, resources, place, and the raw material is tough and difficult to obtain, keeping the business afloat once launched is the trickier part. Most businesses come to an end, not because there is a lack of work, but because they could not manage the finances. Not all are indeed good at numbers and finance, and often, help is required.

People have now understood the importance of managing finances and are eager to outsource business financing. Here enters the role of bookkeepers and financial professionals. With the small business boom, there is also a huge demand for financial management. Our focus is on QuickBooks Bookkeeping and how it is the best way to earn money in 2021. In the following chapter, we will see how much a bookkeeper earns in the US. What services you can provide as a QuickBooks Bookkeeper, and which cities are the best for practicing QuickBooks bookkeeping.

4.1. Salary of Part-Time QuickBooks Bookkeepers

We hear that QuickBooks is a good way to earn money. It is a good side hustle. Be a part-time QuickBooks bookkeeper. No one tells us how much you can make and how much time should be spent to earn a certain amount.

Here we will give you a clear picture of the earnings. A breakdown by weekly, monthly, and yearly earnings.

According to the latest surveys up to 2021, in the United States of America, a QuickBooks bookkeeper's average salary is $50,618 a year. This comes to be around $4,220 per month, around $1000 a week, and about $24 an hour. This sounds very decent for a part-time job. Especially in recent times when we are surrounded by uncertainty, QuickBooks Bookkeeping is a good side hustle.

The figure of $50,618 is the average; it has been reported that you can earn as high as $95,000, and the earnings can even be as low as

$29,000. If you want to look at its percentile wise it will look something like this:

- 90th Percentile earnings $93,500 yearly

- 75th Percentile earnings $ 58,500 yearly

- 25th Percentile earnings $ 36,000 yearly

As the survey is based on all kinds of bookkeepers, from entry-level ones to more professional ones, you see a huge income difference. This also suggests that the more experienced and professional abilities you acquire, the higher you will earn.

The following charts must explain the salaries of part-time QuickBooks bookkeepers in a better way.

- The Yearly Average Income of QuickBooks Bookkeepers

$29,000   National Average $95,000

$50,618 /year

$24 /hour

- The Average Monthly Income of QuickBooks Bookkeepers

- The Average Weekly Income of QuickBooks Bookkeepers

- The Hourly Average Income of QuickBooks Bookkeepers

The following table will give you a better understanding of the earning possibilities that come with QuickBooks bookkeeping. These are the results of a recent survey. Thus, they also indicate the present trends as well.

	Annual Salary	Monthly Pay	Weekly Pay	Hourly Wage
Top Earners	$93,500	$7,791	$1,798	$45
75th Percentile	$58,500	$4,875	$1,125	$28
Average	$50,618	$4,218	$973	$24
25th Percentile	$36,000	$3,000	$692	$17

4.2. The Top 10 Highest Paying Cities for Bookkeepers in the USA

The survey also indicated that the pay varies from location to location. Here we have compiled the top ten cities in the US where QuickBooks Bookkeepers' salaries are higher than the national average.

The state that offers the highest salaries to the QuickBooks Bookkeepers is, without any doubt, California. Companies in California employ the highest paying QuickBooks bookkeepers. The top salaries are recorded from San Francisco, CA. San

Francisco's salaries are around $13,636 higher than the national average. That counts for a whopping 26.9% higher average salary than the average. The second highest is Fremont, CA. The third position is held by San Jose, CA, with a $9,337 higher average salary than the national average of $50,618. Following close behind in Oakland, CA, with an $8,668 higher average. After this is Tanana, AK, with an average yearly salary of $ 59,078, number six is Wasilla, AK, with a higher average of $8459 than the national average. Hayward, CA, has an average income of $58,044 for QuickBooks Bookkeepers. At number eight is Sunnyvale, CA, with an average income higher by $7,268 than the national average. The average salary for this part-time job in Jackson, WY, is $57,870. The last of the tip than in Norwalk, CT.

The table will give you a better understanding of the top ten cities for QuickBooks Bookkeeping.

City	Annual Salary	Monthly Pay	Weekly Pay	Hourly Wage
San Francisco, CA	$64,254	$5,355	$1,236	$30.89
Fremont, CA	$61,596	$5,133	$1,185	$29.61
San Jose, CA	$59,956	$4,996	$1,153	$28.82
Oakland, CA	$59,286	$4,940	$1,140	$28.50
Tanaina, AK	$59,078	$4,923	$1,136	$28.40
Wasilla, AK	$59,077	$4,923	$1,136	$28.40
Hayward, CA	$58,044	$4,837	$1,116	$27.91
Sunnyvale, CA	$57,886	$4,824	$1,113	$27.83
Jackson, WY	$57,870	$4,823	$1,113	$27.82
Norwalk, CT	$57,752	$4,813	$1,111	$27.77

Having mentioned all these cities does not mean that the prospects of getting jobs are higher in these places. This is just an overview of the average income you can earn in these states. Other factors should also be considered when you decide to work in a specific location. For example, you see many six cities from the state of California. You might be tempted to search for work there. But according to research, the job market for QuickBooks Bookkeepers is not active in California. The companies might be paying higher, but the job opportunities are less. It is always smarter to work in a place where the prospects of being employed are better. However, you might be earning more if you locate in one of these locations. It all depends upon the service you provide and the requirements of the employer. It would help if you did your survey before deciding to change your location.

Another important consideration when thinking about making a location change as a QuickBooks bookkeeper is the cost of living. San Francisco may be paying the highest, but the basic cost of living is high. You might be earning more but even spending more on necessities like housing, insurance, and food. This might not prove to be a smart move. For a QuickBooks bookkeeper, an important factor in choosing a location might be the salary and a place with a lower cost of living.

4.3. Best Paying QuickBooks Bookkeeping Jobs in the USA

This is true for any field of practice that your job prospects and earnings increase if you specialize in a specific field. This part will discuss the five types of specialized QuickBooks Bookkeepers who earn higher than the typical part-time QuickBooks bookkeepers. All the jobs discuss earn around $7,683 to $14,935 more than the national average. This makes the values about 14.5% to 29.5% more than a regular QuickBooksbookkeeper's salary. So, it is highly recommended that you try to specialize in a certain domain to improve your higher earnings chances. The five jobs we will be discussing are:

1. CPA Firm Bookkeeper

2. QuickBooks Remote Bookkeeper

3. Telecommute Bookkeeper

4. At home Bookkeeper

5. QuickBooks Consultant

4.3.1. CPA Firm Bookkeeper

The Bookkeeper associated with a CPA firm earns around $65,553 annually. This translates to a $5,463 paycheck each month, roughly $1,261 a week. In this case, you will be charging approximately $31.52 an hour. If you consider it seriously, this is quite a decent earning.

4.3.2. QuickBooks Remote Bookkeeper

This job fetches you a whopping $64,952 annual earning. This is more than $14,300 than the national average. You will be earning $5,413 per month, which is decent.

4.3.3. Telecommute Bookkeeper

According to the survey, the Telecommute Bookkeeper earns $60 795 per year. This is $10,000 higher than the national average. This brings you a decent paycheck of $5,000 per month and weekly earnings of $1,000 plus. Working as a telecommute bookkeeper, you will be charging approximately $30 by the hour.

4.3.4. At Home Bookkeeper

The best thing about this type of bookkeeping is that you can practice it from the comfort of your house, and you will be earning good money. You will be making savings on the commute time, fuel expenses, and outside food expenses, if you practice work from home. Continuing from home, you will still be earning $8,000 more than the national average. You will be earning around $5,000 per month from the comfort of your home.

4.3.5. QuickBooks Consultant

As a QuickBooks consultant, you can earn $57,986 per year. The good part about this is that you can work part-time and take home a paycheck of around $5,000 each month.

This table will give you a better understanding of the benefits of specializing and the financial prospects related to it.

Job Title	Annual Salary	Monthly Pay	Weekly Pay	Hourly Wage
CPA Firm Bookkeeper	$65,553	$5,463	$1,261	$31.52
Quickbooks Remote	$64,952	$5,413	$1,249	$31.23
Telecommute Bookkeeper	$60,795	$5,066	$1,169	$29.23
Work From Home Bookkeeper	$58,536	$4,878	$1,126	$28.14
Quickbooks Consultant	$57,986	$4,832	$1,115	$27.88

Chapter 5. Becoming a QuickBooks Bookkeeper

Now that you have a thorough understanding of bookkeeping and QuickBooks, it must be clear that in present times the knowledge of QuickBooks is essential if you want to work in the US small business community. Sometimes learning the software is not enough. To get the job, you require to show some qualifications and expertise as well. Unfortunately, we are still living in the workplace where showing your qualifications and certificates is essential to acquire a job. But when we talk about QuickBooks, there is no harm in doing a certification. Doing a certification will open many opportunities for you. No one wants to hire an unqualified person. With this Certification, you will be considered qualified for the job. The Certification might teach you the software's basics, but the actual learning is always done practically. Nevertheless, gaining this Certification is beneficial even if it gives you a head start.

Sometimes you have this clear picture in your mind regarding what you want to do but you have no access to proper guidance. Many people want to work as bookkeepers and want to learn further to upgrade their skill set but there is no one to guide them. The information around us is so much that sometimes we are overwhelmed by the excess of information rather than its lack. Sometimes all we need is a plain simple instruction in the right direction. This chapter does just that. It will push you one step further in the right direction.

In this chapter, we will discuss how you can gain this Certification, how much it cost, how long it takes to become certified, the difficulty level of this Certification, the types of certifications available for QuickBooks; all will be discussed in this chapter. In this chapter, we will discuss:

- The type of investment required for Certification.

- Different courses available

- Information about QuickBooks Certification.

- The course fees.

- The duration of the course

5.1. The Type of Investment Required for Certification

Getting a certification is a big investment. Not only are you investing your money, but you also invest your time and money in such courses as well. In present times, the world is ever-changing and keeping up with the fast-moving times has become mandatory. Otherwise, you will be left behind. Similarly, if you are a bookkeeper,you must upgrade your skillset. You might be employed right now, but what if the employer changes technology and you are no more required to work for him/her, and they hire a person with better qualifications. For such times it is important to be well prepared and keep up with times. Your aim should be to become an asset to the company rather than a liability.

5.2. The Different Courses Offered

There are three types of courses offered for QuickBooks Certification. Two of them are for the QuickBooks Desktop, and one is for QuickBooks online. Nowadays, most people prefer a cloud-based financial management system, so it would be wise to take the Certification for the online version. The different types of certifications offered are:

- QuickBooks Online Edition: Basic

- QuickBooks Desktop Edition: Basic

- QuickBooks Desktop Edition: Advanced

5.3. Information About QuickBooks Certification

If you are working as an employee, getting a QuickBooks certificate will reassure your employer of your abilities with the software and convince them that you are an asset to their company. Certification will enhance your credibility. This will equip you with the expertise to deal with any situation that involves QuickBooks. You will be in a better position as a QuickBooks certified employee to tackle tricky situations involving QuickBooks.

When you pass the exam, you will gain the following skills, and your certificate will be proof of your abilities:

- Easily use the main measures of QuickBooks and manage business accounts on the software.

- You can manage all the accounting functions like Payroll, transactions, invoices, and sales smoothly with QuickBooks software.

- Can solve and manage complex scenarios that come up while using QuickBooks.

One thing you should keep in mind, the certifications are not cheap, they cost high prices. But you should consider investing in this Certification as a step towards your better career. You will get profits from this investment very soon.

5.4. Why Should You Invest

It is a known fact that QuickBooks Certifications do not come cheap. If you are an employer, you might feel that this is a lot of investment, and the courses are time-consuming. If you have many employees, the cost might be an issue for sure. If you are a freelance bookkeeper, the fee might be a big investment. But consider this a useful investment. This is one of the investments you should make. Some business owners consider it an initial investment, and the profits and dividends are gained when the work is done more efficiently and faster.

A lot of groups are offering QuickBooks certification courses. If you are an employer, you can look for bundle package discounts and monthly packages. If you are a freelance service provider, you should look for packages that offer monthly installments as one-time payments are sometimes difficult to pay at once.

You should always look for online courses. Nowadays,many online courses are available, and you can take them from the comfort of your home or office. This can save you the commute expenses and the time which is wasted with the commute. Always look for certifications with live tutoring. These sessions are more interactive, there are live questions and answers sessions, and you learn more this way.

You should be convinced not to take up a QuickBooks certification. If you are still not convinced, maybe this is not for you. But if you want to further your career in bookkeeping, this Certification is essential.

5.5. The Certification Fee

Most bookkeepers follow the method that they do their training from a tutor and then take the certification exam. Two groups conduct the Certification:

- Intuit, through their ProAdvisor Program

- NBA (National Bookkeepers Association)

Intuit is the maker of QuickBooks, and they conduct the test for free. However, they cover their cost by making you purchase the mandatory membership, which is hundreds of dollars. You will have to become a member to get access to the test.

NBA conducts the other Certification. This is a much affordable option. If you decide to take the test through them, the fee is $150 for the ones who are taking the test for the first time. This fee includes a practice test and the actual test. At successful completion, you get a certificate. The certification must be updated every year. The fee for each subsequent year is around $75.

5.6. The Length of Courses

There is no specific length for courses. The courses and workshops are carried out by professionals who specialize in QuickBooks software. The Certification is only a 2-to-4-hour program. If you are already familiar with the software, you might just book your test and pass. But for someone, the learning might take from weeks to months. All this depends upon few factors:

- Do you have basic knowledge about the software?

In this case, if you have basic knowledge and take the test straight away, the chances are that you might not be able to gain Certification. It would be best if you had more than basic knowledge to pass the Certification. You should not take these exams lightly. Since these exams are expensive, you should prepare your best before taking the exam to get greater chances of passing.

- The Certification you might wish to do.

So, there are different certifications offered. In the Desktop version certifications, there is a basic certificate and an advanced certificate. As the name indicates, the advanced certification will be harder and thus require more expertise.

- When you decide to take the test

You must be responsible when you decide the date to take the test. Do not take the test before you are fully prepared. If you decide the test date before proper preparation, the chances are that you might not be able to pass.

Mostly, the tests can be completed in one sitting. The level of the exams is according to the Certification you wish to do. It is recommended to get the basic Certification before you try to obtain an advanced certification.

Chapter 6. Hacks and Tricks for QuickBooks

With every software, you should know about the tricks and tips to make your work more efficient and streamlined. The same is the case with QuickBooks. You can use the experience of others to better your work. You must have heard the term; time is money, and these tips and tricks save your time. And by saving time, they save your money. In present times we are blessed with technology, and we should try to benefit from t as much as possible. The lives we lead in present times are quite stressful, and the work-life balance is frankly off-balance. In such a situation, it is wise to take as much help as possible. That help can be from technology, or you can even benefit from others' experiences and mistakes. Here we will discuss some hacks and tricks the professionals from the field have agreed upon and shared with everyone to benefit from. Here is a list of a few tricks and hacks to make your work quicker and easier.

The trend of 2021 is focused more on cloud-based QuickBooks software. In this chapter, we will discuss the tips and tricks we can apply in QuickBooks Online to gain better results. We have compiled a list of six hacks that you might find helpful:

- Cash receipts should be created.

- Use attachments.

- Use keyboard shortcuts.

- Automate the emails.

- Use QuickBooks Online to track the time.

- Always use the bank rules

6.1. Cash Receipts Should be Created.

It is always a good idea to organize your working space. The same is the case with finances. If you have your cash receipts created and recorded, you will easily overview all money received at any time. With QuickBooks Online, you can enter the details in the sales center and review the records anytime you want. This is a feature of QuickBooks online, which is easy to use and convenient for financial tracking.

- Usage

How you will create cash receipts is simple, go to the sales transactions and create a file med cash receipts. Next, go to the filter list and go to 'Money Received' and enter the date appropriately.

(Cash Receipt Usage)

6.2. Use Attachments

This is a hack that is overlooked a lot of the time, and most people ignore using it. The hack is to attach all related forms and documents to the vendor accounts to be managed at once. For example, you can attach a W-9 to the vendor's account.

(Using Attachments)

So, when you use attachments, you can also attach the bank accounts' files and the credit card details and statements. When all the documents are attached and compiled in one place, they will be easy to review. Another pro tip will be to use naming conventions. This will make the work more streamlined and easier to track. According to experts, not using attachments wastes time you could be spending on other activities. There is no need to work so hard if you have applications in your software that make your work easier and smoother to operate. If you are using a mobile version of QuickBooks online, you can even take a screenshot of any receipt and attach it to the folder. In the same way, you can even attach the invoices and enter the yearly or monthly estimates. If you have the add-on of QuickBooks Payments, you can even receive payments.

6.3. Use Keyboard Shortcuts

This is also a huge time saver. When you are working on multiple things, clicking from one program to another makes everything confusing. The same is the case with QuickBooks. When you are managing multiple entities, you need to work fast, and shortcuts are a lifesaver. Following is a summary of all the important shortcuts found within QuickBooks.

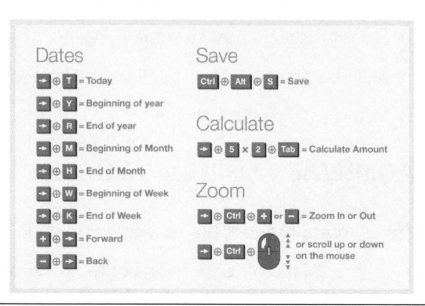

(QuickBooks shortcuts)

6.4. Automate the emails.

For all the regular payments and receiving, automation is the way to go. You should automate your emails for sales, financial statements, and invoices. You must be thinking about how to go about this? It is easy; you will first set different reports scheduled to email on a specific date. For example, you can set a schedule that emails you your financial statement monthly. You can even get an email for the collection report, and the sales report every week. This will help you keep track of the open invoices.

Apart from this, you can schedule the payments that have to be sent out weekly or monthly. You can arrange for the recurring invoices to be sent automatically by email. Again, if you use the app QuickBooks payments, the received payments can be automatically recorded automatically.

6.5. Use the QuickBooks Online to Track Time

If time tracking is tough for you, the newer versions of QuickBooks Online will help you. In the older versions of the program, you had to import the T reports to QuickBooks. In the newer versions, you can create the T sheets within QuickBooks online. These are the integrated T sheets. This means that any change, addition, or deletion would apply automatically to the T sheet, and it will be updated by itself. You will not have to manually update the information. This process is carried out in a seamless manner. You can create several employee T sheets and even approve several T sheets simultaneously.

6.6. Always use the Bank Rules

This is a simple and logical hack. The bank rules are already made, and time tested. If you implement them and set your regular payments to the utilities, vendors, suppliers, etc., on bank rules, the task will become easier. This can save a lot of time for you as well. At the end of the month, all you will need to do is an overview of all the payments carried out in a smooth and streamlined fashion.

These hacks and tips may seem simple but implementing them can save you hours and hours' worth of labor. There will be far fewer things on your mind. It is a one-time setup, and it will be automated from then on. You will easily manage the payments, receiving, employee timesheets, Payroll, and everything else with ease, and you will become less stressed.

Chapter 7. QuickBooks Usage in Small Businesses

Many small businesses use QuickBooks to manage their finances. The software takes care of their bill payments, monitors their cash flow, and manages invoices. QuickBooks is a good software to generated automated monthly financial reports as well as yearly financial reports. Some business owners manage their accounts themselves and are pro users of the software, but most business owners employ professionals to manage their accounts. QuickBooks certified bookkeepers are employed by small to mid-size business owners to manage their accounts.

Small business owners use QuickBooks for several functions and use. Following are the functions for which the small business owners use QuickBooks:

- Make and track invoices.

- Monitor expenses and other bills.

- Generate business and financial statements.

- Manage payroll.

- Do the inventory.

- Simplify taxes.

- Online payments.

- Record Receipts.

- Manage mileage.

7.1. Make and Track Invoices

The software has the option to create invoices, and you can easily print them or directly send them to your customers. Each invoice generated by the software will be automatically recorded in the system. In this way, you can track all the amount that has already been paid, and the receivables will also be displayed.

7.2. Monitor Expenses and Other Bills

You have an option to link the QuickBooks software to your accounts and credit cards. This will enable the program to record all payments and bills automatically and keep a record. It will be available for your view whenever you require.

You can enter other bills you receive in the system and take care of the payables. This will help you keep track of your expenses and payables. The software will make sure you do not miss your payments. If you attach the QuickBooks payment app, the payments can even be managed automatically.

7.3. Generate Business Financial Statements

The software can generate financial statements that will give you an overview of your business performance. The kind of statements you can generate with the QuickBooks software are:

- Cashflow Statement

- Profit and Loss Statement

- Balance Sheets

7.4. Manage Payroll

The software can manage the Payroll and working hours of each employee automatically. You must create a separate account for each employee, enter each employee's information, and schedule the salary, deductions, schedules, and hours. All can be managed automatically by the software. If you use the software, you can easily manage:

- Payment to the employees can be made by checks or cash.

- The taxes can be deducted automatically, and the tax-exempt employee payments are also managed.

- The software fills tax forms automatically

- The payroll taxes can be managed automatically.

7.5. Do the Inventory.

The software manages the inventory. It records the quantities and keeps track of the total cost of inventory. The software will indicate when the inventory is getting low, and there is a need to replenish. This all is not done automatically, you will have to enter the amounts manually, but they will be managed and calculated automatically.

7.6. Simplify Taxes

Taxes is one of the most difficult parts of the business. Most people are fearful of taxes, and in the end, their taxes are piled up.

QuickBooks takes care of your taxes. The Tax becomes difficult because your financial statements are not in order. QuickBooks makes the financial statements simplified, and you can easily print them out and let a tax preparer assess the statements and use the required information.

7.7. Online Payments

The QuickBooks Payments app enables you to accept payments directly from your customers. This app is integrated into the software, so all the payments are recorded in the system automatically.

7.8. Record Receipts

The QuickBooks app makes it possible for the business owner to upload all the payment and expense receipts to the software, and they can be easily scanned and recorded in the system.

7.9. Manage Mileage

If you use your vehicle for business purposes, a tax deduction is applied. But to receive the tax deduction, you will have to prove your traveling. You get a deduction of 57.5 cents per mile. To record the miles, you can link QuickBooks Online to your vehicle's GPS, and it will easily record your miles, date, and time

Write a sneak peak on how to earn passive income with crypto

What is passive income?

Trading or making an investment in projects is one way to make cash in the blockchain enterprise. However, that usually calls for designated research and a sizeable investment of time – however it nonetheless receivers guarantee a reliable source of earnings.

Even the great traders can revel in prolonged periods of loss, and one of the methods to continue to exist them is to have alternative resources of income.

There are different techniques than buying and selling or making an investment that allows you to growth your cryptocurrency holdings. These can pay ongoing income just like earning hobby, but most effective require some effort to set up and little or no effort to hold.

This way, you can have several streams of income that could add as much as a sizeable quantity in aggregate with each other.

This article will go through some of the methods that you could earn passive profits with crypto.

What are the ways you can earn passive income with crypto?

Mining:

Mining essentially manner the usage of computing electricity to comfy a community to receive praise. Although it does no longer require you to have cryptocurrency holdings, it's far the oldest method of income passive profits inside the cryptocurrency space.

In the early days of Bitcoin, mining on a regular Central Processing Unit (CPU) was a possible answer. As the community hash fee multiplied, the maximum of the miners shifted to using more powerful Graphics Processing Units (GPUs). As the competition elevated, even greater, it has nearly exclusively turn out to be the playing field of Application-Specific Integrated Circuits (ASICs) - electronics that use mining chips tailor-made for this precise reason.

The ASIC enterprise is very aggressive and dominated by way of groups with extensive sources to be had to install on research and improvement. By the time these chips arrive at the retail marketplace, they may be in all likelihood already outdated and could take a large amount of mining time to interrupt even.

As such, Bitcoin mining has typically turn out to be a corporate enterprise in preference to a feasible supply of passive income for a median character.

On the opposite hand, mining decrease the hash rate Proof of Work coins can still be a profitable undertaking for a few. On those networks, using GPUs can nonetheless be possible. Mining lesser-acknowledged cash deliver a better ability reward however include higher hazard. The mined cash would possibly become nugatory overnight, bring little liquidity, experience a Trojan horse, or see themselves hindered by using many other elements.

It is well worth noting that putting in place and retaining mining gadgets calls for an initial funding and a few technical expertises.

- **How to Mine Bitcoins**

Miners are becoming paid for his or her work as auditors. They are doing the paintings of verifying the legitimacy of Bitcoin transactions. This convention is supposed to maintain Bitcoin user's sincerity and changed into conceived by way of Bitcoin's founder, Satoshi Nakamoto. By verifying transactions, miners are helping to prevent the "double-spending problem."

Double spending is a scenario wherein a Bitcoin owner illicitly spends the equal bitcoin twice. With bodily forex, this isn't an issue: once you hand a person a $20 invoice to shop for a bottle of vodka, you not have it, so there is no threat you could use that identical $20 bill to buy lotto tickets round the corner. While there is the possibility of counterfeit coins being made, it isn't exactly similar to literally spending the identical greenback twice. With digital forex, however, because the Investopedia dictionary explains, "there is a danger that the holder ought to make a replica of the digital token and send it to a service provider or some other birthday celebration at the same time as preserving the authentic."

Let's say you had one valid $20 invoice and one counterfeit of that equal $20. If you were to try to spend each the actual invoice and the fake one, someone that took the trouble of looking at both of the bills' serial numbers would see that they had been the equal quantity, and accordingly one in every one of them needed to be false. What a Bitcoin miner does is similar to that—they test transactions to make certain that users have not illegitimately attempted to spend the same bitcoin two times. This isn't always an ideal analogy—we will explain in more detail beneath.

Once miners have confirmed 1 MB (megabyte) well worth of Bitcoin transactions, referred to as a "block," the ones miners are eligible to be rewarded with an amount of bitcoin (extra about the bitcoin reward below as nicely). The 1 MB restriction became set by means of Satoshi Nakamoto, and is an issue of controversy, as some miners believe the block size needs to be increased to house greater statistics, which might effectively imply that the bitcoin network could process and verify transactions faster.

Note that verifying 1 MB well worth of transactions makes a coin miner eligible to earn bitcoin—not all and sundry who verifies transactions will receive a commission out.

1MB of transactions can theoretically be as small as one transaction (although this isn't always at all common) or numerous thousand. It relies upon how a whole lot of facts the transactions soak up.

"So in the end that paintings of verifying transactions, I would possibly nonetheless no longer get any bitcoin for it?"

That is accurate.

To earn bitcoins, you need to fulfill two conditions. One is an issue of effort; one is a matter of success.

1) You must verify ~1MB really worth of transactions. This is the easy part.

2) You ought to be the primary miner to reach the right solution, or closest solution, to a numeric hassle. This system is likewise known as evidence of work.

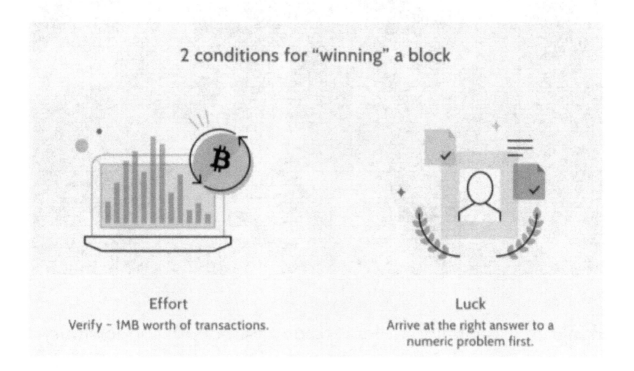

2 conditions for "winning" a block

Effort
Verify – 1MB worth of transactions.

Luck
Arrive at the right answer to a numeric problem first.

Staking:

Staking is essentially a less resource-in-depth opportunity to mining. It normally involves preserving finances in a suitable pocket and acting various community functions (together with validating transactions) to get hold of staking rewards. The stake (meaning the token conserving) incentivizes the protection of the network's protection through ownership.

Staking networks use Proof of Stake as their consensus set of rules. Other versions of it exist, which include Delegated Proof of Stake or Leased Proof of Stake.

Typically, staking entails setting up a staking wallet and simply maintaining the coins. In a few instances, the procedure includes adding or delegating the price range to a staking pool. Some exchanges will try this for you. All you need to do is hold your tokens at the trade and all the technical requirements could be taken care of.

Staking may be a wonderful manner to grow your cryptocurrency holdings with minimal effort. However, some staking projects hire strategies that artificially inflate the projected staking returns charge. It is essential to research token economics models as they could correctly mitigate promising staking praise projections.

Binance Staking supports an extensive variety of cash with the purpose to earn you staking rewards. Simply deposit the cash on Binance and comply with the manual to get started.

Lending:

Lending is a very passive way to earn interest in your cryptocurrency holdings. There are many peer-to-peer (P2P) lending platforms that permit you to lock up your funds for a time period to later gather interest payments. The interest charge can either be fixed (set through the platform) or set via you primarily based on the cutting-edge market price.

Some exchanges with margin trading have this feature implemented natively on their platform.

This technique is ideal for lengthy-time period holders who need to boom their holdings with little effort required. It is well worth noting that locking funds in a clever contract constantly carries the threat of insects.

Binance Earn offers a selection of alternatives that assist you to earn hobby on your holdings.

Crypto lending for investors

To make it clearer allow's take an example: You are the satisfied proprietor of 10 bitcoins and also you would love to generate a regular passive income along with your bitcoins. By depositing these 10 bitcoins at the pockets of crypto lending platforms, you may receive weekly (or monthly) pastimes from it. For bitcoin lending, these hobby charges typically are from three% to 7% at the same time as they can be loads better (up to 17%) as an example on the more strong property such as stablecoins (e.G. USD Coin, True USD, Binance USD).

And what is even more exciting with those funding types in comparison to others including peer-to-peer lending, ii's that with crypto-backed lending, borrowers should stake their personal cryptocurrency as protection and ensures mortgage repayment. So in case, the borrower makes a decision now not to pay off the loan, the investors can just promote the cryptocurrency belongings to cover the loss.

Naturally, every now and then borrowers don't repay their loans. But due to the fact funding platforms require debtors to stake 25 to 50% of the mortgage in crypto, structures are commonly capable of getting better most of the losses and avoid traders losing cash.

Crypto lending to borrow

So we mentioned all this as an funding, but allows not forget the borrowing side of it!

If you are studying this text, you are maximum probable to believe in the future of crypto. Thus retaining your crypto for the long term is vital.

Cryptocurrency lending permits you to borrow physical money (e.g. USD, EUR, CAD) while you need it in order to avoid having to promote your crypto in case of an emergency.Jef wef

How crypto lending works?

Who is involved?

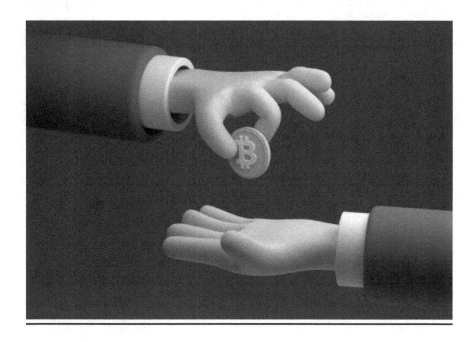

Lenders and borrowers in cryptocurrency lending are linked through a 3rd celebration, in this example, an online crypto lending platform, which acts as a relied-on middleman.

So, for this form of lending to take place, there should be 3 events involved: lenders, debtors, and lending systems:

•   The lenders or buyers who want to lend crypto. This will be someone holding cryptocurrencies anticipating the price to soar (HODL-ers), or just a crypto aficionado seeking to grow his assets' output.

• The crypto lending platform takes care of the transaction related to lending and borrowing. When it involves these systems, we've got decentralized platforms, self-sustaining platforms, and centralized structures with a group of individuals or corporations working at the back of the curtains.

• The borrowers trying to gain price range for something purposes. This may be a person or an enterprise searching out investment and need to use crypto or fiat assets as collateral with a purpose to get funding.

Detailed steps of the process

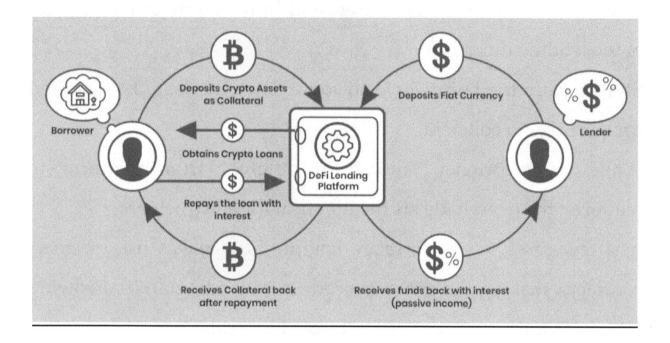

Step 1: The borrower taking place a platform are requests a crypto mortgage (backing it up with his crypto)

Step 2: Once the platform every day the loan request, the borrower stakes his crypto collateral. The borrower won't be able to get lower back the stakes amount till he funds back his entire loan.

Step 3: Investors (lenders) fund the mortgage robotically through the platform. Usually, this technique is invisible for traders for whom the stability of crypto on their accounts could be unchanged.

Step 4: Regularly pursuits are paid to investors (normally on a weekly or month-to-month bases, and infrequently at the give up of the lending duration).

Step 5: Once the borrower paid lower back the loan, he acquired back his crypto collateral.

While cryptocurrency lending is different from platform to platform, the overall idea is the identical for all structures.

In a few cases, cryptocurrency lending also makes use of smart contracts, making the entire procedure of lending and borrowing safer in that the contract itself enforces the terms.

Running a Lightning node:
The Lightning Network is a 2d-layer protocol that runs on top of a blockchain, which includes Bitcoin. It is an off-chain micropayment network, which means that it can be used for instant transactions that aren't right now transferred to the underlying blockchain.

Typical transactions on the Bitcoin network are one-directional, which means that if Alice sends a bitcoin to Bob, Bob cannot use the equal payment channel to send that coin back to Alice. The Lightning Network, but, uses bidirectional channels that require the 2 individuals to agree on the terms of the transaction ahead.

Lightning nodes provide liquidity and growth the potential of the Lightning Network with the aid of locking up bitcoin into charge channels. They then collect the expenses of the payments running through their channels.

Running a Lightning node may be a project for a non-technical bitcoin holder, and the rewards heavily rely on the overall adoption of the Lightning Network.

Affiliate programs

Some crypto businesses will reward you for purchasing extra customers onto their platform. These include affiliate links, referrals, or a few different bargains provided to new customers who are introduced to the platform by using you.

If you have got a larger social media following, associate packages may be an exceptional way to earn some facet profits. However, to avoid spreading the word on low-pleasant tasks, it is constantly well worth doing some research on the services ahead.

If you are interested by earning passive profits with Binance, be a part of the Binance Affiliate Program and get rewarded while you introduce the arena to Binance!

Masternodes

In simple phrases, a master node is similar to a server however is one which runs in a decentralized community and has functionality that different nodes on the community do no longer.

Token projects have a tendency to provide out unique privileges simplest to actors who have a excessive incentive in retaining community balance. Masternodes usually require a substantial prematurely funding and a considerable amount of technical expertise to set up.

For some masternodes, however, the requirement of token holding may be so excessive that it efficiently makes the stake illiquid. Projects with masternodes additionally tend to inflate the projected go back costs, so it is constantly important to Do Your Own Research (DYOR) before making an investment in a single.

Forks and airdrops

Taking benefit of a difficult fork is a exceptionally truthful tactic for traders. It merely requires preserving the forked cash on the date of the hard fork (commonly decided by block top). If there are two or more competing chains after the fork, the holder will have a token balance on every one.

Airdrops are much like forks, in that they best require ownership of a pockets deal with on the time of the airdrop. Some exchanges will do airdrops for his or her users. Note that receiving an airdrop will never require the sharing of personal keys - a condition that could be a telltale signal of a rip-off.

Blockchain-primarily based content material introduction structures

The creation of dispensed ledger technology has enabled many new kinds of content material platforms. These permit content material creators to monetize their content material in several specific approaches and without the inclusion of intrusive commercials.

In this kind of device, content material creators maintain possession of their creations and normally monetize attention in a few way. This can require plenty of work first of all but can offer a constant source of earnings as soon as a more massive backlog of content material is ready.

What are the risks of earning passive income with crypto?

Buying a low-best asset: Artificially inflated or misleading go-back rates can lure investors into shopping an asset that in any other case holds little or no value. Some staking networks undertake a multi-token system in which the rewards are paid in a 2nd token, which creates steady promote stress for the praise token.

• **User errors:** As the blockchain industry remains in its infancy, putting in place and preserving these assets of earnings calls for the technical know-how and an investigative mindset. For a few holders, it might be best to wait till those services grow to be greater person-pleasant or best use ones that require minimal technical competence.

• **Lockup periods:** Some lending or staking techniques require you to fasten up your finances for a fixed amount of time. This makes your holdings efficiently illiquid for that point, leaving you prone for any occasion which can negatively affect the charge of your asset.

• **Risk of bugs:** Locking up your tokens in a staking pocket or a clever agreement always contains the chance of insects. Usually, there are a couple of choices to be had with numerous degrees of pleasure. It is imperative to analyze these selections before committing to one. Open-supply software might be a very good place to begin, as the one's options are a minimum of audited by way of the network.

Closing thoughts

Some ways to generate passive income in the blockchain enterprise are growing and gaining reputation. Blockchain corporations have additionally been adopting some of those strategies, presenting services commonly referred to as generalized mining.

As the products are becoming extra reliable and relaxed, they might soon become a legitimate alternative for a consistent supply of profits.

Conclusion

If you have read the whole book, many of your doubts must have been cleared regarding bookkeeping and QuickBooks. This is an amazing opportunity for you to avail yourself if you want to take up bookkeeping as a profession. It is always a better idea to keep up with the current trends and technology because it ensures better job and working opportunities. Therefore, we have mentioned QuickBooks. Being a QuickBooks certified bookkeeper gives you an edge in business. This is because most small to mid-size businesses have installed the QuickBooks software for their financial management. There are different versions of QuickBooks available:

- QuickBooks Self-Employed

- QuickBooks Online

- QuickBooks Desktop

- QuickBooks Apps

QuickBooks is user-friendly and is compatible with other programs like MS Word and MS excel. Different versions are available that are compatible with iOS, android, windows, and Mac operating systems.

It will be a good idea to specialize in cloud-based QuickBooks software because, as of 2014, more and more business owners are interested in keeping their records on the cloud-based package offered by QuickBooks. If you are planning to get your Certification any time soon, the cloud-based product should be your focus. There is a basic course offered in QuickBooks Online; you should consider that.

Another consideration when thinking about QuickBooks bookkeeping seriously is what type of Bookkeeper you are going to be. According to a survey, these five types of part-time QuickBooks bookkeepers are making the highest number of average incomes:

- CPA Firm Bookkeeper

- QuickBooks Remote Bookkeeper

- Telecommute Bookkeeper

- At home Bookkeeper

- QuickBooks Consultant

The next most important point to think about is your location. At different locations in America, bookkeepers make different yearly incomes. The QuickBooks bookkeepers make the highest yearly earnings in San Francisco, California. But before quickly packing your bags towards the sunny state, keep in mind the expenses as well. Before shifting your location, always consider the basic expenses and how you will be managing them. It may be possible that you are earning less in one city, but the cost of living is cheaper, and in another city, you might be making more money, but the expenses are equally higher. In the latter case, you end up losing more money. So, always take a well-thought-out and informed decision.

In all, if you are someone good with numbers and have a consistent work ethic, you can very manage to be a QuickBooks bookkeeper. You can even work as a freelance service provider. Providing services is also generally a risk-free approach. The only investment you make is the training you do and the courses you take. After that, all is gain. In this way, you can set your schedule and take up as much work as you can manage. In present times where the future has become unpredictable, freelancing is the way to go.

CPSIA information can be obtained
at www.ICGtesting.com
Printed in the USA
BVHW011454180821
614614BV00009B/478